Life's Emotional

Journey

How Relationships Affect
Our Mental Health

GABRIELLE KALLUS

Gotham Books

30 N Gould St.
Ste. 20820, Sheridan, WY 82801
https://gothambooksinc.com/

Phone: 1 (307) 464-7800

Published by Gotham Books (December 11, 2024)

ISBN: 979-8-3306-0352-7 (P)
ISBN: 979-8-3306-0353-4 (E)

Because of the dynamic nature of the Internet, any web addresses or links contained in this book may have changed since publication and may no longer be valid.

The views expressed in this work are solely those of the author and do not necessarily reflect the views of the publisher, and the publisher hereby disclaims any responsibility for them.

I dedicate this book to my children as well as all those who have been a part of my life. Without you there would be no reason for creating this book!

TABLE OF CONTENTS

PART I: *Relationships*

PART II: *Emotional Relationships*

Foreword

This book is about what we go through in life with regards to acceptance, rejection, and love. We each have our own unique experiences with acceptance, whether it is to accept ourselves as we are, or gaining acceptance from others. The first section of the book relates what we go through in each of these cycles, because that is what they are. The second section relates to the mental health issues that can occur as a result of the ways we are accepted, rejected, or loved within the many types of relationships we have in our lives.

****

A little bit about myself: I grew up in a small town. I had sustained a bad traumatic brain injury when I was 2 ½ years old. I was diagnosed with a learning disability at that point, as well as epilepsy. As a result of this injury, I questioned God many times about why I had been injured. I had a difficult time accepting why for many years. So I have gone through self-acceptance issues many times throughout my journey, and I want you to know that you can get through the challenges that your journey brings.

I knew early on that my survival meant that I had a purpose. I have gone way past what any doctor believed I would ever do—I graduated high school on time, went on to college, and finally I went on to graduate school and obtained a master's degree in psychology.

Writing this book has been a therapeutic process for myself as I have gone through acceptance, rejection, and love, as well as mental health issues. I hope you get as much out of this book in reading it as I have had in writing it!

PART I

Relationships

The Journey Begins

We all have needs. Abraham Maslow (1908-1970) created a hierarchy of various needs that we have throughout life. This hierarchy of needs includes five levels of needs, and these needs build upon each other, from the most basic needs on up to self-actualization. These needs include physiological needs, safety, love and belonging, esteem, and self-actualization. Maslow believed that we needed to focus on the first needs—our physiological needs, which include food, water, and clothing, and safety, which would include shelter and stability—prior to focusing on the higher needs of love and belonging, esteem, and self-actualization (West, M., 2022, www.medicalnewstoday.com). Love and belonging includes relationships and acceptance. Esteem relates to self-confidence and respect from others. Finally, self-actualization occurs when we reach out potential and achieve our goals.

Anthony Robbins (Taylor, J., 6 Core Human Needs by Anthony Robbins, www.habitsforwellbeing.com) suggests that there are six core needs that we as humans have. He suggests that success and happiness "can be found by meeting certain needs that are fundamental to human beings" (Taylor, J., 6 Core Human Needs). Included are certainty, variety, significance, love and connection, growth, and contribution. The first four needs (certainty, variety, significance, and love and connection) are defined as "needs of the personality," while the last two needs (growth and contribution) are seen as "needs of the spirit" (Taylor, J., 6 Core Human Needs).

Although Robbins' core human needs are somewhat similar to Maslow's, Robbins also covers more area in that uncertainty is added to the equation. I believe that by combining the needs that Robbins identifies with the needs that Maslow finds that are necessary for our physiological and psychological well-being, that we can become more fully in tune with ourselves and satisfy our human needs effectively. We tend to believe that love is an automatic when we are born, but it doesn't always happen due to circumstances beyond our control. I believe that by combining the needs that Robbin identifies as essential with Maslow's hierarchy of needs, that we can become more fully in tune with ourselves and satisfy our human needs more effectively.

If we do not get that love and that sense of acceptance and belonging from early on, we have no way to know how to give love and how to accept others. Life can get better if you have the acceptance in your life that you need, and you can get there even if you have not had the acceptance from day one. However, if you did not experience love and acceptance early on, there is still hope!

You can learn these qualities well past your childhood years! The purpose of this book is to help you understand this need.

Why are love and acceptance so important to us? Why is it so important for us to be liked, to be accepted, to be loved? What has social media done to us that we feel we must be liked or we are nothing? As social beings--especially since we as people learn to like, love, dislike, and even hate others--we want to be liked. We are on social media hoping for others to like what we say or do. We voice our opinions in hopes of finding others who believe in similar ways. We want to belong to something greater than ourselves. Being accepted and loved also is important to our psychological well-being. When we do not have the love and acceptance that we yearn for, several things begin to happen to us. First, our self-esteem plummets. Second, chemical changes occur in the brain, and we go into survival mode. Third, our thinking becomes distorted and we begin to feel that we are not worthy of anything that is good. Finally, because of all these changes, various mental health issues can develop, including depression, anxiety, and suicidal thoughts, among others.

There are so many people in the world who have never felt loved or accepted, those who have been rejected all of their lives. They feel bad about themselves because they are different, or maybe they were unwanted. They want to be the same as everyone else. But this is where we have it wrong. It is okay to be different.

3

However, it is also difficult to be different because acceptance does not come easily for someone who is different in either a physical or mental capacity.

Friendships are beneficial for those who have mental health issues. How is this? Normally, those with mental health issues become more isolated because they do not feel that they are accepted within a group anymore. However, if you have some truly accepting friends, their friendship and support can help you to overcome, or at least improve, some in regard to your mental health (www.mentalhealth.org.uk). Many times, however, the mentally ill person is skeptical of whether or not they are truly accepted, so the mental illness lingers and may even worsen because of this belief.

It feels good to know that there are differences in the world, and even though we are different, we can accept others even if they have a different view. That is what has makes life so challenging, so fun. I can accept you as a person even if you and I have differing political or religious views. I have a friend that is completely different than me in their values and beliefs. However, I can respect his beliefs even if they are different than mine. But there are many out here that feel so strongly about something that they cannot see other people's opinions as valid, even if there is a lot of evidence to support the other person's belief.

One person I know has had it rough since day one. He was the product of an extramarital affair, so his stepfather was abusive toward him from early on. He tried to gain acceptance of his stepfather by joining an organization that his stepfather was a member of, but acceptance never came from his stepfather. It has taken him years to get past the abuse, even though his stepfather is no longer alive. The stepfather's other children were abused by him as well, but nothing like the torment that he put my friend through.

As for myself, I have my own story. Because I began at a public school and transferred to a parochial school, I found myself to not be accepted by the other girls in my class. My first friends were two boys in my class. Later on, when some new girls transferred from another town, I made sure to befriend them right away because I knew how it felt to not be accepted. Friendships blossomed with these two new students, but years later, in junior high, no amount of acceptance by these two friends could stop the bullying that occurred. In seventh grade, there was a student that bullied me because even though I was learning, I was not learning at the same pace as everyone else, all because of the traumatic brain injury I had obtained when I was 2 ½ years old. Many years later, when my youngest son was in second grade, he had his catechism class in that exact same room, and every time I took him to class, I had a major anxiety attack. Unfortunately, I was the only licensed driver in the family at the time, so it was up to me to get him to class. Many years later, I finally was able to forgive that classmate, 35 years later!

Being accepted into a group gives a person a sense of belonging. The first group we are all a part of is the family. Many times, however, that first group makes us feel like we don't belong, like we were accidents, unwanted. This can really take a toll on the person! Although there may be a genetic marker for the development of mental illness, it is that first feeling that we do not belong that brings about the changes that occur that can create an organically created mental illness. The psychological consequences are so great that if the general public knew what was happening, I believe that each family would become more accepting of the baby right away. Acceptance and love go hand in hand. One cannot have one without the other. Accept others from day one and help them to become the best people they can become!

A very good friend of mine gave me a book of Bible passages when I was in jail. Little did she know that the day she gave it to me, I was in the lowest of moods. I really needed this book that day. That book covered a wide array of topics, and I have found it most helpful in my life journey since then. I still refer to this book often when I am struggling with a difficulty.

Rachel Hollis (2018) stated something that I completely agree with about life: "Your life is supposed to be a journey from one unique place to another; it's not supposed to be a merry-go-round that brings you back to the same spot over and over again" (xiv-xv). So, where will you go on this journey we call life?

My parents could have never imagined the journey they would be placed on, experiencing the death of one child and nearly losing another, but they did as well as they could given the circumstances. Never could they have imagined the journeys their children, grandchildren, and great grandchildren are walking on! Much like you never knew where your journey would take you! But we are in this journey we call life together! It is up to us to make the best of it and become all that we can be!

Biblical Study

I believe in God, and God has been an important part of my life. As part of this book, I have added a section to each chapter called Biblical Study. I will reference biblical passages that relate to the chapter topic, and a brief explanation of what each passage means to me.

We begin with some passages about journeys. That is what life is—a journey through the unknown. We each have goals along this journey we call life. Many times we don't know where our life is leading us, but we have to trust that we will get to where we are supposed to be.

The first journey that I think of when I think about the unknown is the journey that God sent the Israelites away from Egypt, to the promised land. Exodus 3:7-10 is where God commissions Moses for this journey.

"But the Lord said: I have witnessed the affliction of my people in Egypt and have heard their cry against their taskmasters, so I know well what they are suffering. Therefore I have come down to rescue them from the power of the Egyptians and lead them up from that land into a good and spacious land, a land flowing with milk and honey, the country of the Canaanites, the Hittites, the Amorites, the Perizzites, the Girgashites, the Hivites, and the Jebusites. Now indeed the outcry of the Israelites has reached me, and I have seen how the Egyptians are oppressing them. Now, go! I am sending you to Pharaoh to bring my people, the Israelites, out of Egypt" (NABRE, 2010).

Moses had no idea what he was getting into. All he knew was that he needed to get his people out of Egypt. He had no idea how long the journey would take, or even that he would die before reaching the promised land.

Do we ever truly know where we will end up? I never knew that I would ever get arrested or serve probation. It was not in my plans, but I feel that it was part of God's plan for me, so that I could reach out to you.

"Accept one another, then, just as Christ accepted you, in order to bring praise to God. For I tell you that Christ has become a servant of the Jews on behalf of God's truth, so that the promises made to the patriarchs might be confirmed and, moreover, that the Gentiles might glorify God for his mercy" (Romans 15:7-9a; NIV). Jesus and God accepted us all, so we should accept one another.

Another journey that you may be familiar with are the journey of Mary and Joseph when they went to Bethlehem to be counted in the census. Mary was quite pregnant at the time, and since they could not find any rooms available, they were given a room in a building much like a barn. This is where she gave birth to Jesus, in humble surroundings.

Things to Think About

What can we do to make others feel accepted and loved? How can we help others to feel wanted and loved? How can we help those that have been abused how to behave appropriately? What can you do to show others that you accept them as they are, that they do not have to change for you or anyone else? What can we do in order to help ourselves when we feel we don't belong? Get to know the person. More than their name, rank, and serial number.

By getting to know the person more deeply, on a more personal level, you are able to pass judgment on what you do or do not like about the person, and if the person is someone you want to have in your life. Where will this life journey take you? What can you do to change the direction your life is going?

Self-Acceptance

Self-acceptance is one of the toughest challenges we have in life. We all have things we do not like about ourselves, things that we can and cannot change. If we work on the things we can change, and accept the things we cannot change, we will become happier and will likely be accepted by others as well. I cannot change the past, but I can change who I have become by working on things that can be changed.

One prayer that most of us know at least the first three lines of is The Serenity Prayer, which was written by Reinhold Niebuhr. However, here is the complete prayer:

God, Grant me the serenity to accept the things I cannot change,

The courage to change the things I can,

And the wisdom to know the difference.

Living one day at a time,

Enjoying one moment at a time;

Accepting hardship as a pathway to peace;

Taking, as He did, this sinful world as it is,

Not as I would have it;

Trusting that He will make all things right if I surrender to His will;

That I may be reasonably happy in this life

And supremely happy with Him

Forever in the next. Amen. (www.beliefnet.com)

Think about that! We all want to be accepted by our peers, but we need to accept ourselves first, work towards peace within ourselves, accept that hardships are part of life, and trust that what we are going through is part of our journey with God! Groups such as Alcoholics Anonymous use this prayer to begin their groups so that those in the group can focus on why they are at the meeting.

What are things that you cannot change? What are things that you can change within yourself, things that you don't like, that you can improve on? What do you like about yourself? I don't like that I have a head injury. However, I cannot do anything about this. I can, however, become a better person, be more accepting of others, and even help others to heal mentally. I like that I am a kind and giving person.

Jennifer Williams (2018) felt that "without self-acceptance, there is no true freedom" (www.blog.heartmanity.com). Self-acceptance means that we accept ourselves unconditionally, acknowledge both our strengths and weaknesses, and are aware of how we can and do influence others. In practicing acceptance and self-love with ourselves, we get ourselves out of the rut of loneliness, since acceptance and self-love are the opposite of loneliness. By accepting ourselves completely, we are able to feel comfortable with ourselves. We are comfortable within our own skin. We are able to be by ourselves without worrying about needing someone else to complete us, since we are comfortable with ourselves. Although I cannot change the fact that I have a head injury, I can become a better person, accept myself as I am, be more accepting of others, and help others accept themselves and help them heal mentally.

Is there a way that we can work on our own self-acceptance? YES!!! It is a type of therapy called Acceptance and Commitment Therapy (ACT). No, you do not have to go through therapy to do it, but you must be open to what you will find out while doing ACT. There are two major goals in ACT: a) "actively accepting unwanted and perhaps uncontrollable thoughts and feelings, and b) commitment and action towards goals that are aligned with one's chosen values" (Sharp, 2012, 360). This therapy works on six particular areas that enable us to refocus on life, and accepting and working toward positive change.

a) Cognitive defusion enables us to reduce the repetition of thoughts, sensations, and emotions.

b) Acceptance allows us to experience the thoughts, sensations, and emotions without resistance.

c) Contact with the present moment allows us to be in the moment and receptive to the here and now.

d) Self as context allows us to observe ourselves objectively.

e) The person then decides on their values, what matters to them the most. It could be anything from friendship, family, money, or any number of things that matter to the person.

f) Finally, the person commits to action that is congruent with the person's values (Sharp, 2012, pp.360-361).

Williams (2018, blog.heartmanity.com) suggested a way to "connect with your authentic power." There are six steps to "quiet mental chatter and connect to your authentic power:

a) Identify a repetitive thought that you say to yourself continuously.

b) Ask yourself, "Is what I'm saying to myself true?"

c) If you answered yes, then ask "How is this thought true?" If you answered no, ask "Why isn't it true?"

d) Next, shift your perception to support how you would like to feel.

e) Then, mindfully look at how you would think and feel differently to feel the way you desire.

f) Take one action to change the way you feel—just one!

What are some ways to accept ourselves? First, don't criticize yourself. Say you are trying something new for the first (or second) time. You have watched others do the skill, and you think that you can do it, but when you attempt the skill, like riding a bicycle, you find that you have difficulty with it. You lose your balance. You fall and skin your knees. You're mad that you cannot do it right the first time. But remember, as a baby you took a tumble many times when learning how to stand and to walk. You didn't give up. Each skill takes time to learn. The phrase "Practice makes perfect" is a good thing to keep in mind because it helps you to remember that not everything can be done right the first time. Were you able to cook a meal perfectly the first time? Even with following the directions from a recipe it is not always easy to do everything right. I remember the first time I tried to make chicken and dumplings! It was a complete disaster! There was no moisture left in the pot, and it was more like a stir-fry rather than a soup mixture! I eventually got it right, but not until I worked at it several times. Not until after you have practiced a skill for a while will you be able to tell yourself either "I've got it!" or "I give up!"

Coping Skills

Coping skills are things we do to help us deal with life's difficulties. There are both positive and negative coping skills, and whichever skills we utilize will determine whether or not the problem continues or dissipates. I will first go over positive coping skills, and then proceed to explain negative coping skills.

Positive coping skills help us to adapt in a meaningful way to whatever situation we are involved with. Included are skills such as breathing slowly, counting to ten, listening to music, writing, going for a walk, meditation, talking to a friend, and facing the problem (www.morningsiderecovery.com).

Negative coping skills, on the other hand, do not allow us to become better people. Negative coping skills include things such as substance abuse (both drug and alcohol are included), avoiding others or avoiding reminders of the trauma that they faced, anger, violence, dangerous behavior, and being hypervigilant (constantly watching out for oneself in an otherwise safe situation) (www.spacioustherapy.com).

I cannot change the fact that I had a traumatic brain injury as a child. That is a fact. I cannot change this fact, but I can change how I react to this fact of my life. I was discouraged a lot as a child because I didn't feel that I was able to keep up, and I didn't feel like I belonged to the class I was in, even though we were all the same age. However, I was able to overcome a lot of the difficulties I had by exercising my brain, my hand/eye coordination, and continually reading and doing other activities. I still have some difficulties that linger, mental health issues as well as some slowness in the brain as a result of this injury, but for the most part no one would know unless I told them. I look "normal," walk, talk, drive, and take care of myself. I push myself further than most people just to prove that I can do the things that others do. I accept that I had this injury, but I push myself further. I attempt to improve myself in any way that I can.

I have found that reading and writing are the ways that I can work best with the brain that I have. Others find that painting, drawing, sewing, and other crafts are good for them, but we each need to find whatever hobby we enjoy the best. I draw and sew as well, but they are hobbies. I don't do them that often. What are things you want to do that will help you become a more independent, stronger individual? What are changes you can make to become who you believe you are capable of becoming?

I found an acceptance prayer on www.bayart.org that I want to share with you:

I accept myself completely.
I accept my strengths and weaknesses, my gifts and shortcomings,
my good points and my faults.

I accept myself completely as a human being.

I accept that I am here to learn and grow, and I accept that I am learning and growing.

I accept the personality I've developed, and I accept my power to heal and change.

I accept myself without condition or reservation.

I accept that the core of my being is goodness, and that my essence is love, and I accept that I sometimes forget that.

I accept myself completely, and in this acceptance I find an ever-deepening inner strength.

I accept my life fully and I open to the lessons it offers me today.

I accept that within my mind are both fear and love, and I accept my power to choose which I will experience as real.

I recognize that I experience only the results of my own choices.

I accept the times that I choose fear as part of my learning and healing process, and I accept that I have the potential and power in any moment to choose love instead.

I accept mistakes as a part of growth, so I'm always willing to forgive myself and give myself another chance.

I accept that my life is the expression of my thought, and I commit myself to aligning my thoughts more and more each day with the Thought of Love.

I accept that I am an expression of this Love. Love's hands and voice and heart on earth.

I accept my own life as a blessing and a gift. My heart is open to receive and I am deeply grateful May I always share the gifts that I receive fully, freely and with joy.

This prayer is very much a prayer for self-acceptance, and helps us to focus on the different facets of ourselves, allowing us to really think about and consider everything within us. What are things that you need to accept about yourself, things you need to get past? What are things we can change about ourselves? What are things we cannot change?

Biblical Study

Self-acceptance is sometimes difficult because we do not like what we see in ourselves. We feel unattractive, so we diet or buy more attractive clothes. We don't like the house we have, or the car that we drive, so we work harder to earn the money so we can get something new. But self-acceptance is more than superficial exterior stuff. It is also about loving who we are inside. Have you ever wondered about why God chose Mary to be the mother of Jesus? He chose her because she was pure in heart and soul. He had created her for the purpose of giving birth to His son. Even though we are all considered to have the stain of original sin upon us at birth, God had created Mary to be without sin. Luke 1:26-38 goes into detail about when the angel Gabriel visited with Mary and informed her that she would conceive Jesus, the son of God.

"In the sixth month, the angel Gabriel was sent from God to a town of Galilee called Nazareth, to a virgin betrothed to a man named Joseph, of the house of David, and the virgin's name was Mary. And coming to her, he said, 'Hail, favored one! The Lord is with you.' But she was greatly troubled at what was said and pondered what sort of greeting this might be. Then the angel said to her, 'Do not be afraid, Mary, for you have found favor with God. Behold, you will conceive in your womb and bear a son, and you shall name him Jesus. He will be great and will be called Son of the Most High, and the Lord God will give him the throne of David his father, and he will rule over the house of Jacob forever, and of his kingdom there will be no end.' But Mary said to the angel, 'How can this be, since I have no relations with a man?' And the angel said to her in reply, 'The holy Spirit will come upon you, and the power of the Most High will overshadow you. Therefore the child to be born will be called holy, the Son of God. And behold, Elizabeth, your relative, ha also conceived a son in her old age, and this is the sixth month for her who was called barren; for nothing will be impossible for God.' Mary said, 'Behold, I am the handmaid of the Lord. May it be done to me according to your word.' Then the angel departed from her" (Luke 1:26-38; NABRE, 2010).

So Mary accepted that she, a virgin, would become the mother of Jesus, the son of God. She accepted that she would bear this child who would become a religious leader.

There are other stories of acceptance. One in particular is the story of Abraham. Abraham was tested by God through the sacrifice of his son, Isaac. Abraham set everything up and then placed his son on top of the pile of wood. As he was about to sacrifice his son, an angel of the Lord called Abraham and stopped him from killing his son. He was then provided with a ram to sacrifice instead (Genesis 22:1-19).

Truly all of the New Testament is a story of acceptance because people of many backgrounds were accepted into the fold as followers of Jesus, including tax collectors, Samaritans, Jews, and Gentiles, among others. We are all unique. No one, not even an identical twin, is completely like another person because we each have our own personalities. Jesus even accepted the particular type of death that he was to suffer even though he did not want to die.

Things to Think About

Work at a new skill to become the new and improved you! One new skill at a time! Others won't notice the change till you have learned several new things, but keep it up and prove to yourself that you are capable of doing more things than people give you credit for! Don't give up on learning something new! Accept this new part of you!

While this chapter is about self-acceptance, what are things that you can do to show acceptance of those who are different than you?

Being Alone vs. Being Lonely

Being alone is not a bad thing. It is a way to pursue your dreams, find out who you are without the influence of others, and becoming who you want to be. Who are you? Who am I? Over the last year I have learned a lot about being alone, and a lot about being lonely as well. There is such a difference in mindset! Being alone, without my children or a partner, has made me learn how to take care of myself, rather than being mom and taking care of others rather than me. Do I like all the responsibilities? No way! But we all have to learn that there are things that we need to do that we do not necessarily like.

Being alone means you are comfortable being by yourself (part of self-acceptance), and being lonely means that you are uncomfortable being by yourself and even in the presence of others because you feel that you are not accepted. **Remember: Being alone is not a bad thing. It is a great way to know what we accept and reject about ourselves! By finding out what we like and dislike about ourselves, we can find what we can change to become the person we want to be.** But remember, change is not easy, and there are those in our lives that will not like the changes that we make. Stay strong, though, so you can become everything you are meant to be!

We need to feel comfortable by ourselves, but it is when we are not comfortable being by ourselves that problems begin. Do you know people who are comfortable with themselves? Those that feel like they can be who they are with or without others? It's not easy. Loneliness steps in because we are uncomfortable with who we are. We feel uncomfortable with those who we are "supposed" to be close to because we are different than those we feel we are supposed to be close to. We take on everything by ourselves because we don't feel comfortable leaning on others. Loneliness creeps in and takes over. I have a friend that I have repeatedly leaned on when I feel out of control (Thank you, Patty!). I sometimes wonder if she reconsiders when I ask for help, but she has never turned me down.

If you are anything like me, and I dare say that most of you are, you try to avoid being alone. My children are not with me at this time, and being alone means I have felt many times that I have no purpose (at least that is how I have felt recently), so I fill my time with talking to people online, getting to know others, and helping those that need help. This is probably not the most healthy habit, but it keeps me communicating with others, making me feel that I mean something to someone. Then there are times, like now, that I am here thinking about what I want to tell you that makes being alone not so bad. So often we don't want to be alone because it allows us to think about why we like the things we do, why we enjoy being with others, and why we pursue others in the hope of them filling our lives with comfort. Yes, comfort! It is comforting to know that someone is there for us! It is comforting to know we do not have to go through life alone! Having someone in our lives means we have a built-in support system (emotional as well as financial).

Being Alone

Being alone is beneficial to ourselves both mentally and spiritually. How is it beneficial? One website, www.powerofpositivity.com, points out nine important reasons why being alone is good for you:

a) Being alone clears the mind.

b) Being alone fosters creativity.

c) Being alone builds confidence.

d) Being alone encourages independence.

e) Being alone clarifies perceptions.

f) Being alone diminishes stress and anxiety.

g) Being alone establishes priorities.

h) Being alone boosts productivity.

i) Being alone strengthens relationships

(www.powerofpositivity.com).

Being alone rejuvenates us mentally, increases our faith in our abilities, and allows us the ability to grow mentally, spiritually, and emotionally because we are putting ourselves first instead of someone else. Yes, it is good to put yourself first! It is actually beneficial if you decide to make yourself a priority! If you are not in good health mentally or physically you certainly cannot be there for others emotionally! Does that make sense to you? By putting yourself first, you are allowing yourself to become healthy enough to increase your mental and emotional strength so you can help others when you are able to! When you slow down and make yourself a priority, you allow yourself to become more focused on what you need. Being alone is healthy for the person. It helps you to become your full self, the one who is capable, understanding, and creative. When you become your true self, the best comes out in you, and you begin to believe that you are able to do more, and you become a better example for those around you.

By putting yourself first, you are allowing yourself to become healthy enough to increase your mental and emotional strength so you can help others when you're able to! Taking care of yourself is not selfish! It is essential!

Loneliness

Loneliness is different than being alone. One can be lonely by themselves or even in a group of people. Loneliness is defined as being "destitute of sympathetic or friendly companionship, intercourse, support, etc." (www.dictionary.com). Loneliness happens because we need to connect with others but are unable to. We are social beings. This connection does not have to be with a human. That connection can be with caring for a child or a pet. That is why so many times when you tell someone that you are lonely, the person will recommend an activity or to get a pet. That way purpose becomes a part of the lonely person's life.

Having a purpose allows the person to feel important, that they are needed in some way, a reason why being active within a church or other social organization is often seen as a positive way to get past loneliness and depression. Being needed is essential in order to feel fulfilled.

But one can be lonely even in a group of people if one feels no emotional connection or support from the group. Often, the lonely person just wants to be included and to feel important to someone else. If you are a member of a group or organization, it is necessary that you feel that you are an important part of the group. If you are a member of a group but have made no substantial effort to contribute, such as voicing an opinion, you can still feel lonely.

The reason loneliness feels so bad is because we do not feel important to those who mean something to us, be it family or friends. If we don't feel important, we become depressed or anxious. Getting depressed means that our ability to function in the workplace (at work or at home) goes down. Depression can mean different things to different people. For myself, I tend to internalize my feelings, and instead of reaching out to others, I stop doing chores around the house. Then, I get more depressed and overwhelmed because I realize it is something I cannot handle on my own, and I break down. Others may use washing dishes or changing the sheets as therapy, knowing that once they have a chore done they will feel better. It all depends on the severity of the depression, and whether the depression is short-term or long-term.

Anxiety is another mental health disorder that happens frequently when we feel lonely because we are asking ourselves, "Why doesn't someone like me? Why am I not accepted?" Because we are asking ourselves the questions, and not another person, and ruminating on the question, we become anxious. I have both depression and anxiety, and even though I know what I need to do to get out of these moods, I can much more easily tell you, the reader, how to deal with these issues. Both depression and anxiety will be discussed more in depth in later chapters.

According to Gretchen Rubin (2017, www.psychologytoday.com), there are seven types of loneliness: a) New situation, b) I'm different, c) No sweetheart, d) No animal, e) No time for me, f) Untrustworthy friends, and g) quiet presence. Even though there are so many different types of loneliness, Rubin (2016, www.gretchenrubin.com) suggests several habits that we can do in order to combat loneliness: a) Nurture others, b) Connect with other people, c) Get better sleep, d) Stay open, and e) Ask yourself "What's missing in my life?"

In doing research for this book, I found several ways in which being alone and being lonely differ. Because loneliness brings about isolation, we feel emotionally abandoned, empty inside. We want so bad to feel better that we attempt to find distractions to fulfill us, and many times these distractions are not fulfilling because we are yearning for something deeper, some emotional connection. We blame ourselves, yet we also are depending on someone else to bring happiness to us when what we really need to do is provide our own happiness (Joshi, 2015; www.storypick.com). Rubin (2009, www.gretchenrubin.com) found several factors that makes loneliness so difficult for the person who feels lonely. First, "loneliness sets us apart by making us more fragile, negative, and self-critical." Second, they are less accepting of potential new friends when they are lonely. Third, when they are in class, they are less responsive in class and give less effective feedback than non-lonely students. Fourth, they tend to be more aggressive, more self-defeating, or less cooperative, and less likely to think clearly. Finally, those who are insecure and anxious tend to identify with television characters more than real people.

Loneliness in itself is unhealthy for us physically and mentally. "Chronic loneliness significantly increases our risk of cardiovascular disease. Loneliness suppresses the function of our immune system. College freshmen who felt lonely had poorer reactions to flu shot" (Winch, G., 2014, 10 Surprising Facts About Loneliness). So it is to your benefit to work at maintaining social relationships, friendships, and staying connected with others. One way to help yourself while helping others is to attempt to socialize with someone else who looks to be lonely. That way you are helping both yourself and the other person. Or get a pet that needs to be taken care of so that you have a purpose.

Social relationships occur when people who have similar interests begin to know one another. As a result of these social relationships we are able to gain confidence within our belief system, build personal and professional relationships, and find out who we can rely on in times of need, those that we are comfortable talking with. Being socially active helps us with our physical health as well because those who are socially active "live longer and are healthier than their more isolated peers" (Umberson and

Montez, 2010). There is a link between social isolation and health conditions such as cardiovascular disease, hypertension, and cancer (Umberson and Montez, 2010). By accepting others as they are, and finding others that accept us as we are, we will be able to more fully heal from the difficulties we had in our earlier years. Acceptance of ourselves is very important, not just from ourselves, but from others!

Biblical Study

Being alone is not a bad thing. It allows us to think, to discover new things about ourselves, and even to help us decide who we are. There are many passages in the Bible about being alone. The first one is near the very beginning, in Genesis 2:18-24.

The Lord God said: It is not good for the man to be alone. I will make a helper suited to him. So the Lord God formed out of the ground all the wild animals and all the birds of the air, and he brought them to the man to see what he would call them; whatever the man called each living creature was then its name. The man gave names to all the tame animals, all the birds of the air, and all the wild animals; but none proved to be a helper suited to the man. So the Lord God cast a deep sleep on the man, and while he was asleep, he took out one of his ribs and closed up its place with flesh. The Lord God then build the rib that he had taken from the man into a woman. When he brought her to the man, the man said: 'This one, at last, is bone of my bones and flesh of my flesh; This one shall be called 'woman,' for out of man this one has been taken. That is why a man leaves his father and mother and clings to his wife, and the two of them become one body (Genesis 2:18-24, NAB).

Although Jesus had many followers, there were times when even he would need time alone. After he had healed the leper, he took time to be by himself. Luke 5: 15-16 states: "The report about his spread all the more, and great crowds assembled to listen to him and to be cured of their ailments, but he would withdraw to deserted places to pray" (NAB). Taking time to be by yourself is healthy because it helps you to rejuvenate.

Loneliness is also discussed in the Bible. In the book of Joshua, God speaks to Joshua. This book is written not long after the death of Moses. Joshua has served as Moses' aide for many years, and so now Joshua has to step up into a leadership role. God's words are comforting to him (Joshua 1: 5-9):

No one can withstand you as long as you live. As I was with Moses, I will be with you: I will not leave you nor forsake you. Be strong and steadfast, so that you may give this people possession of the land I swore to their ancestors that I would give them. Only be strong and steadfast, being careful to observe the entire law which Moses my servant enjoined on you. Do not swerve from it either to the right or to the left, that you may succeed wherever you go. Do not let this book of the law depart from your lips. Recite it by day and by night, that you may carefully observe all that is written in it; then you will attain your goal; then you will succeed. I command you: be strong and steadfast! Do not fear nor be dismayed, for the Lord your God, is with you wherever you go (NABRE).

In this passage, it is clear that God will always be with his people, that he will be there in times of happiness and in despair, so that his people will never be lonely.

The book of Psalms has many passages that speak of loneliness, but one particular passage is actually the entirety of Psalm 27:

The Lord is my light and my salvation; whom should I fear? The Lord is my life's refuge; of whom should I be afraid? When evildoers come at me to devour my flesh, these my enemies and foes themselves stumble and fall. Though an army encamp against me, my heart does not fear; though war be waged against me, even then do I trust. One thing I ask of the Lord; this I seek: To dwell in the Lord's house all the days of my life. To gaze on the Lord's beauty, to visit his temple. For God will hide me in his shelter in time of trouble, he will conceal me in the cover of his tent; and set me high upon a rock. Even now my head is held high above my enemies on every side. I will offer in his tent sacrifices with shouts of joy; I will sing and chant praise to the Lord. Hear my voice, Lord, when I call; have mercy on me and answer me. 'Come,' says my heart, 'seek his face'; your face, Lord, do I seek! Do not hide your face from me; do not repel your servant in anger. You are my salvation; do not case me off; do not forsake me, God my savior! Even if my father and mother forsake me, the Lord will take me in. Lord, show me your way; lead me on a level path because of my enemies. Do not abandon me to the desire of my foes; malicious and lying witnesses have risen against me. I believe I shall see the Lord's goodness in the land of the living. Wait for the Lord, take courage; be stouthearted, wait for the Lord (NABRE, 2010)!

Even when we feel the loneliest of all, God will be with us. We can call on him even in our darkest hour!

Things to Think About

Remember: Being alone is not a bad thing. We need to feel comfortable by ourselves, but it is when we are not comfortable being by ourselves that problems begin. Being alone is not a bad thing, but not having any social relationships is bad. What can you do to feel more comfortable being alone? Are there things that you could be doing to help ease the feeling that creeps in called loneliness? What project can you do to keep your mind off of feeling lonely? What can you do to build social relationships and become healthier in the process?

Acceptance

Self-acceptance is so important to the health and well-being of you, but acceptance from others is also very important as well! It is that feeling that you are accepted and loved by others that makes life worth living. I enjoy writing, but right now it is not being accepted by family members as a way to cope. It is what I have turned to, in the last year particularly, to express myself.

In my previous book, I touched briefly on the topic of love and acceptance. It is such an important topic that I am devoting this book to love, acceptance, and rejection. The late psychologist Abraham Maslow wrote about the hierarchy of needs. The hierarchy of needs is usually displayed as a pyramid, with the base needs of clothing, food, and shelter as a purely basic physical necessity. This in general would be true to the extent that we need each of these things in order to physically survive. However, I would argue that the most basic psychological needs that we all have--love and acceptance--are just as important as the physical needs. Why? There are so many people alive in this world who have been unwanted, who have been unloved, and have not been able to learn to recognize what true love and acceptance is. Without love and acceptance, we are many times denied the food, clothing, and shelter that we so desperately need. Living without love and acceptance is just survival.

Megan Bruneau (www.mindbodygreen.com) found that we have the choice to accept or reject someone or something. This is what makes rejection so utterly painful, because we realize that we are not in control of how others see us, and that they can choose whether or not to accept us as people. What, then, is acceptance exactly? Bruneau suggested several facets to acceptance: a) Acceptance does not mean liking, wanting, choosing, or supporting. b) Acceptance is an active process. It must be practiced. c) Acceptance doesn't mean that you can't work on changing things. d) Acceptance doesn't mean you're accepting is going to be that way forever. e) We can practice acceptance toward our experience, people, appearance, emotions, ideas, and more.

Bruneau (www.mindbodygreen.com) and Williams (2018) seem to have conflicting ideas on whether or not choice is part of the equation. However, if I may explain, their definitions do not conflict. Yes, we do choose whether or not to accept something. However, Bruneau does not mean that we do not choose to be accepting. Rather, she is stating that accepting is more of a cognitive reassurance of what is real, such as the fact that you have a limitation that is concrete. We can choose to accept people and ideas, but we do not have a choice on whether or not to accept a permanent change to our physical being. It either is or is not.

Several years ago my father had to have a leg amputated because of an infection or else he was going to die within days. Although losing his leg was not his choice, he managed to accept the loss of the leg and even went so far as to learn how to function with the use of a prosthetic leg. He can still do most activities, although there may be some limitations to what he can do. He has accepted the loss of the limb as part of his life, but he continues to live and function almost as well as he used to when he had both legs.

Belonging to a group, whether it is in a classroom setting, a social group, or a team, makes one feel accepted and important, like their opinion matters. The first group we are ever a part of, though, is family. So often we feel like we belong, but then something happens and our personal needs go to the side. The acceptance is gone.

What if the social group you belong to needs you to do something, like donate money towards purchasing food, and you have nothing that you can give? You can easily feel used, like the financial needs of the group are being put before the needs of each individual. So you drop away from the group. One or two members might ask you why you left, since it was a group you normally enjoyed being a member of. You tell them that you felt that it was being required of you to contribute financially when you had nothing to give. This gives them something to think about, and they actually make the effort to get you to be active in the group again, by asking those that can give, to please do so, and that it is not a requirement as part of the group. They figure out ways that you can contribute without having to come out of pocket. What can you do to contribute to the group? That purpose gives you all the more reason for staying in the group. Having a purpose makes one feel important, like the person is necessary.

Love and acceptance. Why do I put them together so much? It is because if you are loved, then you are accepted. But love is not the same as acceptance. Acceptance can be done without loving someone. I accept that there are others who have different viewpoints than me, but do I love them completely? No. That is conditional love. I love them because they are people, but it does not go further than that. I knew, growing up, that I was loved by my parents and sisters. They accepted me as I was, but honestly it was not without condition. I grew up with my own opinions, my own views, and while they did not understand why I felt the way I did, they still accepted me. Sometimes we are accepted until we can no longer be of help to someone. I had this happen to me recently, and it hurt that the person did not love enough to stick around. But I learned that the person did not truly love me. They just loved me for what they thought I could do.

Acceptance is extremely important, especially as a child. A lot of times we want to feel accepted by others that are not our family. We want to have friends, people that accept us for who we are. A teacher of mine—Patty—accepted me into her kindergarten class a couple of weeks into the school year. I had already begun attending a different school prior to entering her class, but the other school did not have the faculty to help with my learning needs, so they recommended my going to the other school. What she saw in me was quite different than what the other school saw. She saw a happy, respectful student who just needed some extra help. With her classroom being half the size of the other school's classroom, she was able to help me to learn more easily. She made it easier for me to learn, and made sure that I felt accepted by her. Although she had accepted me, it was still a real struggle because I also wanted to be accepted by my new classmates. The only ones I felt accepted by were two boys that allowed me to play with them. They were my best friends for several years. When new girls came to the school, however, I made sure to befriend them so that they did not experience the same loneliness I felt when I first came to the school.

Let's go back to the earlier example of acceptance. You feel that you cannot contribute much as a member because you do not have the financial means to contribute to the group. Because other group members made the effort to include you, you felt that you were a valuable group member. Your self-esteem went up. But what if no one had made the effort to include you? Your feelings about yourself went down, and you quit doing something you enjoyed. As a result, depression set in and you were unable to function as well as you did previously. I have felt both ways many times. But the thing is, **you are responsible for the way you act and react to those around you. You will either be accepted or rejected because others choose to either accept or reject you, and given that we have been given free will, you probably will not be able to change how someone else sees you. First impressions are pretty difficult to change, so control the way you react to the acceptance or rejection. It is all in how you react.**

Biblical Study

Lack of acceptance is one of the most difficult things to deal with in our lives. Rejection is very painful, especially if we want a certain person to like us. We have to remember that we may not be what the other person wants to have in his or her life. We may not be right for that person.

What does the Bible say about acceptance? "This is how we know what love is: Jesus Christ laid down his life for us. And we ought to lay down our lives for our brothers and sisters. If anyone has material possessions and sees a brother or sister in need but has no pity on them, how can the love of God be in that person? Dear children, let us not love with words or speech but with actions and truth" (1 John 3:16-18; NIV). Loving and accepting others, even in the poorest of conditions, is necessary in order to show our love of God. If we do not accept others, than we have no true love for God.

"Accept the one whose faith is weak, without quarreling over disputable matters. One person's faith allows them to eat anything, but another, whose faith is weak, eats only vegetables. The one who eats everything must not treat with contempt the one who does not, and the one who does not eat everything must not judge the one who does, for God has accepted them" (Romans 14:1-3; NIV).

"Then Jesus declared, "'I am the bread of life. Whoever comes to me will never go hungry, and whoever believes in me will never be thirsty. But as I told you, you have seen me and still do not believe. All those the Father gives me will come to me, and whoever comes to me I will never drive away'" (John 6:35-37; NIV).

Things to Think About

How can we show others that they are accepted by us? What can we work on in order to change so that others are more accepting of us?

Relationships

Relationships are very important! Why are they so important? It is through the relationships we have with others that we learn who we are as people and what makes us happy. We learn what our passions are in life, how we feel about important topics (Have you watched the news and felt an urge to tell off someone?), and we find out who will be in our lives through both the good and bad times.

Types of Relationships

There are so many types of relationships! There are friends, enemies, business partners, love relationships, social relationships, marriages, singles, committed, and so many others! But how do we begin with any type of relationship? We get to know each other. Family, of course, is the first relationship most of us have. We are born into or adopted into a family. It is expected that there is a love between the parents and the child, but unfortunately not everyone will feel the love from the parents. Yes, this is a negative aspect for the child brought into this family, but they can learn to love from other people, even if the love is not felt immediately.

Carl Rogers (1902-1987) initially wrote about what it takes to build a good therapeutic relationship, but he went a step further later in showing how the same facets that are vital in a therapeutic relationship are just as important in an interpersonal relationship, the type most of us attempt to build throughout life. What are these three facets to a good solid relationship between anyone? First, there needs to be genuineness—what he called congruence—and this genuineness includes being open and honest with a person. By being open and honest about who we are, and where we have been, the other person learns about why we are the way we are. Congruence, according to Rogers, is "an accurate matching of experiencing and awareness" (Rogers,1961; 339). Next is what he called unconditional positive regard, or acceptance of the person. Basically, we need to put aside all our own personal, political, and religious views in order to understand the person and accept the person for who they are. Finally, Rogers believed that empathy, which is listening and understanding, is very important to any developing relationship, whether it is as a friend, lover, boss, or employee. Once we have these three aspects down, the true development of the relationship can build, whether it be with family, socially, within the work place, or in a therapeutic relationship.

Social relationships are beneficial to our behavioral, psychosocial, and physiological health. How? When we have positive relationships with others, our behavior changes, as well as our thoughts and our physical well-being. The converse is also true. If we do not have good social relationships, our mental and physical health declines, and depending on the trauma experienced, the effect can be very quick, or it can build up over years. Those with a larger social network tend to have better mental health than those who have a very small social network (Umberson and Montez, 2010). However, those with a small social network can also have good mental health because they have figured out who their true friends are and have learned to rely on those few that they do have in their lives.

Family

Family is defined as "a domestic group of people with some degree of kinship—whether through blood, marriage, or adoption. Ideally each child is nurtured, respected, and grows up to care for others and develop strong and healthy relationships" (www.pamf.org). We learn to treat others the way we are treated, so unfortunately many times the abused becomes an abuser. The abused person, unless they develop a close relationship with another family, will never know that the abuse is not a normal part of a relationship. Family makes it possible to form solid, life-long relationships.

What if you do not have the ideal family relationship? Well, you can still learn about how to treat others by observing how teachers treat you and other people, watch how other relationships are among friends, and get a feel for how the people you hang around treat each other. One woman I knew had been abused and raped repeatedly throughout her childhood. She knew it wasn't right, but she was just a child, and did not know how to stop it. She couldn't stop it. Fortunately she was able to stop the cycle when she had her own children. She knew what was right and wrong. However, because of the physical and sexual abuse, and the neglect she experienced as a child, she developed a severe depression.

Someone else, on the other hand, had not experienced the things the previous example had. Instead, she felt a closeness to her family, was not abused, and was generally happy at home. However, her social skills were lacking, and getting to know others was a challenge because she felt different than her classmates. She did not feel the same acceptance that her family gave her among her peers. She developed depression as well as anxiety because of her feeling left out, even though her home relationship was ideal.

As you can see, while not everyone has the same experience, we can all develop in different ways. Our relationships with others may not be ideal. But can we learn from our early relationships? Definitely! Can we make changes in the way we relate to others! YES!!! It takes work, but we are all capable of making positive changes in our lives!

Friendships

Friendships develop like many other relationships. You notice that someone is interested in something that you like, or you want someone to play with, or maybe you are introduced by family. However you meet, there are always reasons you like the person, just as there are reasons that you do not like someone. It is a conditional love more than likely, at least in the beginning—I like you because you are similar to me. Lifelong friendships often begin this way, and as the two people get to know each other, they become more accepting of the quirks the other one has. The lifelong friendship can turn into what is more like a familial relationship. It's not so much I like you because anymore, but rather I like you in spite of these things that others may not like. They value each other.

I have had friendships torn apart because of someone I thought I loved. Although I have mended the friendships with several of these people since then, the friendships are not the same as they once were. We have all become parents and live in different parts of the state, so we are busier than we were as teens and young adults. So even though we are not as close physically as we once were because of distance, we remain friends. Fortunately we are able to understand that we are not the same people that we were before, and that the changes in our lives have allowed us to become better people.

Social Organizations

We become members of social organizations because the organization poses an interest within our lives. It could be a quilting circle, a Lion's Club, Knights of Columbus, or a reading club. Then, after becoming a member and attending a meeting or two, we realize that we know some of these members from other areas of our lives. Our friendships grow deeper because of similar interests, interests that we never knew we had in common. The question is, why did we not know that the other person had an interest in something we liked before? We obviously did not get to know the person as well as we thought we had.

Romantic Relationships

Getting to know another person romantically usually begins because we like how a person looks. Don't lie to yourself. We all do this. Physical attraction comes first the majority of the time. The way a person looks will tell you whether or not you want to know the person romantically, as a friend, or not at all. Unfortunately some of the nicest folks are those who are not so much physically attractive, but attractive because of their personality. So we must give ourselves a chance to get to know the person because of their personality before being a judge of character on whether or not we are attracted to a person.

Frustration within Relationships

Kathleen Smith (2018, When Anger Becomes Emotional Abuse: How to Control Anger and Frustration in a Relationship, www.psycom.net) addresses anger and frustration and suggests several ways to control their reactions:

a) "Avoid the impulse to cut off." What this means is, don't run away, don't slam the door, don't stop listening. Listen to the person in a calm manner.

b) "Focus on managing yourself (and not your partner)." Control your emotions because you are the only person that you can control.

c) "Be aware of triangles." Triangles happen when we share what happened in an argument to another person. That person may or may not have your best interests at heart, and really, they only know your side of the situation.

d) "Look past the issues." There are certain topics that are always hot issues—money, politics, and religion, to name a few. "Rather than getting hung up on resolving conflict as quickly as possible shift your focus back to responding as maturely as you possibly can" (Smith, 2018).

Frustration can be, well, frustrating! If we develop good coping skills and are mature about whatever makes us angry or frustrated, we can salvage a solid relationship rather than letting our emotions take control. It is when our emotions take control that we are most vulnerable to the other person's whims.

Biblical Study

Relationships with others helps us to maintain a more stable mentality. It is not just the love relationship, but also business relationships, friendships, and spiritual relationships, that matter within our lives. If any of these areas is unstable, our mental health will also be unstable.

Jesus made it clear that building relationships was essential to life, to work, and at home. He had a good relationship with both his earthly parents (Mary and Joseph), and he had an ongoing relationship with his Heavenly Father, praying to Him often. He had relationships with the men he called as followers, as well as people within the areas where he preached—some as healer, some as forgiver, some as comforter, but he also had a relationship with society as a leader of faith and as a teacher. He knew what it was like to be liked, loved, hated, and rejected. He suffered the same ailments as sadness, anxiety, and grief filled his heart. Who better to turn to than Jesus, since he experienced many of the same things we do every day?

"Do not let any unwholesome talk come out of your mouths, but only what is helpful for building others up according to their needs; that it may benefit those who listen. And do not grieve the

Holy Spirit of God, with whom you were sealed for the day of redemption. Get rid of all bitterness, rage and anger, brawling and slander, along with every form of malice. Be kind and compassionate to one another, forgiving each other, just as in Christ God forgave you" (Ephesians 4:29-32; NIV). It may be difficult to do this at times, but by treating others the way you want to be treated, you will be showing them that control even in anger can bring about compassion, even to those who may not deserve it.

"You have heard that it was said, 'Love your neighbor' and hate your enemy.' But I tell you, Love your enemies and pray for those who persecute you, that you may be children of your Father in heaven. He causes his sun to rise on the evil and the good, and sends rain on the righteous and the unrighteous" (Matthew 5:43-45; NIV). God plays no favorites!

"Whoever jabs the eye brings tears; whoever pierces the heart bares its feelings. Whoever throws a stone at birds drives them away; whoever insults a friend breaks up the friendship. Should you draw a sword against a friend, do not despair, for it can be undone. Should you open your mouth against a friend, do not worry, for you can be reconciled. But a contemptuous insult, a confidence broken, or a treacherous attack will drive any friend away" (Sirach 22:19-22; NABRE). Friendships can be repaired if there is no malicious attack against the other person. Relationships are essential, whether they be friends, family, coworkers, a date or spouse, or social relationships.

Spiritual relationships are also important. In St. Paul's letter to the Ephesians, he signifies the different types of relationships, first with spouses, parents, then slaves, and then finally with God. "Finally, be strong in the Lord and in his mighty power. Put on the full armor of God, so that you can take your stand against the devil's schemes. For our struggle is not against flesh and blood, but against the rulers, against the authorities, against the powers of this dark world and against the spiritual forces of evil in the heavenly realms. Therefore put on the full armor of God, so that when the day of evil comes, you may be able to stand your ground, and after you have done everything, to stand. Stand firm then, with the belt of truth buckled around your waist, with the breastplate of righteousness in place, and with your feet fitted with the readiness that comes from the gospel of peace. In addition to all this, take up the shield of faith, with which you can extinguish all the flaming arrows of the evil one. Take the helmet of salvation and the sword of the Spirit, which is the word of God. And pray in the Spirit on all occasions with all kinds of prayers and requests" (Ephesians 6:10-18; NIV). This is how our spiritual relationship with God should be! We should be close to the Father, pray for strength, and be ready for when our time in this earthly world comes to an end!

Things to Think About

Relationships are built early on, from the relationship with your parents, to the friendships you build in school, to the people you date. How you treat each person is likely similar in how you have been treated. How do you want to be treated? What type of relationship do you want? Do you just want to know someone socially? Do you want a friendship to develop? Do you want something more romantically? I had a friendship that began first as trying to keep the person from committing suicide. It developed into a friendship that was meaningful to both of us. I developed deeper feelings, but this person did not want this to happen, so I had to rethink what I valued about this person. We took a break from each other for several months and have finally become friends again.

Develop a social network of those that you can trust, those you can rely on in times of need. Knowing who you can depend on, someone to back you up, gives you the confidence that you need. These friends will encourage you in different ways— your professional, personal, and spiritual life can be better just by this network of people that you have. You will also be healthier just by having a support network.

Love

Love has been written about in many ways—songs, poetry, novels, plays, self-help books, even the Bible. With so many ways to write about love and what it is, one would think that there was a standard definition of love. But love is defined in so many ways that no two definitions are alike. One person will say that love is the total acceptance of another person, while others state ways to show love. Another way to define love is in the varying degrees of what people say love is. One author (lonerwolf.com) found that there are eight types of love, while another author stated only seven levels of love (all but mania, which was given on lonerwolf.com). M. Scott Peck (1978) defined love as "The will to extend one's self for the purpose of nurturing one's own or another's spiritual growth" (81).

To understand what love is, we must first understand what it is not, and understand what others think it might be. First of all, love does not hurt. It is not need or attachment, it is not seeking, and it is not grasping. Love is also not simply to want something badly, nor is it desire with the intent to change something or someone else into what we want it to be. Love IS accepting the other person as they are, warts and all, without intent to change the person into what they are not (www.raptitude.com). "To love fully is to love all" (www.raptitude.com). Rabbi David Wolpe (www.timeinc.net) helped redefine how we see love. Instead of love being an intense feeling of deep affection, which is how most see it, he redefined it as an "enacted emotion." Love "expresses itself in action," and is shown by what we do (Wolpe, www.timeinc.net). So in defining love as being expressed through action, we can see what love is not.

So, what is love? In the Bible (NIV) we are instructed by Jesus to "Love one another. As I have loved you, so you must love one another" (John 13:34, NIV). Jesus, as God, has shown us that His love is unconditional. So we are instructed to love unconditionally. Love is defined in 1 Corinthians 13 as: "Love is patient, love is kind. It does not envy, it does not boast, it is not proud. It is not rude, it is not self-seeking, it is not easily angered, it keeps no record of wrongs. Love does not delight in evil but rejoices with the truth. It always protects, always trusts, always hopes, always perseveres. Love never fails" (1 Corinthians 13: 4-8, NIV). While this may define what love is, it is more related to acceptance than to love. If a person is patient and kind to a person, the person is accepting of the person and their limitations. It states how the relationship should be, not exactly what love is. By accepting who the person is, we are able to use the Bible's definition of love as a basis for relationships.

55

There are four types of love in the Bible (www.thoughtco.com): a) Eros, which is sensual, romantic love; b) Storge, which is family love; c) Philia, which is intimate love; and d) agape, which is the highest form of love in the Bible, God's immeasurable, incomparable love for humankind, and is perfect, unconditional, sacrificial, and pure. Other researchers have added more types of love (Burton, www.psychologytoday.com; and www.lonerwolf.com).

However, in order to form good, solid relationships—not just romantic ones—we need to know what types of love there are. The ancient Greeks (yes, even before the Bible!) found that there are eight types of love: a) Eros (erotic love), b) Philia (affectionate love), c) Storge (familiar love), d) Ludus (playful love), e) Mania (obsessive love), f) Pragma (enduring love), g) Philautia (self-love), and h) Agape (selfless love) (www.lonerwolf.com). Burton (www.psychologytoday.com) does not include mania in his description of the different types of love, but does go into detail about the seven other types of love that are mentioned in the article on www.lonerwolf.com.

So many times we just see those who are in the Eros level of love, people who just want to have a physical relationship and nothing more. I don't know about you, but I want a combination of loves—but you cannot give love if you have no self-love. Mental illness, many times, is the result of not feeling good enough, having no self-love. Being in love, or falling in love, is a matter of feeling all these types of love at the same time! Yes, even mania has a place in love. You would do anything to keep the love that this person feels for you (within reason, of course).

According to Thich Nhat Hanh (Brown, L., 2017), "True love makes you happy and makes the other person happy" (www.hackspirit.com, Thich Nhat Hanh on Love). Hanh, a Vietnamese Zen Master, states that there are four elements to true love:

a) Loving kindness
b) Compassion
c) Joy
d) Inclusiveness

All of these elements feed off of each other.

Loving kindness begins when we "are able to generate a feeling of joy and happiness [in ourselves] and are able to help the other person do the same" (Brown, 2017). So, by creating joy and kindness within ourselves, and helping another person to create these same feelings, we are showing loving kindness.

Compassion is shown by "the capacity to make yourself suffer less and help the other person to suffer less as well" (Brown, 2017).

If there is no joy (happiness), then there is no love. If your significant other makes you suffer or cry every day, then love is not there. Joy is generated "for yourself and for the other person" (Brown, 2017). Who causes laughter in your life? What brings joy to your spirit?

Inclusiveness, most of us believe, is including everyone within a group. There are schools that include both mentally and physically disabled students within the classroom with able-bodied individuals who are "normal." This is what most of us think of when we consider inclusiveness. Inclusiveness in the Buddhist definition of love is when you don't see the "frontier between the one who loves and the one who is loved" (Brown, 2017). You do not see where one person's love ends and the other person's love begins. What one experiences, the other will experience as well, because both people understand (are empathic) to the other person's feelings. Your love for the other person will expand, eventually, to include everyone.

Self-Love

What is self-love? It is acceptance of yourself in all ways, or, if you are unhappy with some of the ways you are, it helps you to define what you do not like about you so that you can work to improve or change that aspect of you. Are there things about yourself that you do not like? Except for my weight, and maybe my emotionality, I don't believe I have things I really want to change about myself. But that is just talking about it without thinking about it. What do you want to be like? Is there some way that another person is that you admire? If I sit and think about it, I would like to make more money, be able to be independent and take care of myself and my family. I admire those who are able to find someone and stay with someone for many years. My parents were married for 55 years, and the last 5 or so years my dad was taking care of my mom with the help of some caregivers, so that is the type of love I want. One that is forever.

Love of self, according to Lachlan Brown (2019; www.hackspirit.com/how-to-love-yourself) explains 15 steps to believing in yourself again, which essentially is how to love yourself:

a) "You are absolutely the most important person in your entire universe." By allowing yourself to define yourself as this important person, you first feel better about yourself, albeit a little guilty for putting yourself first.
b) Be kind to yourself, be patient, and forgive yourself. Some ways you can do this are by taking care of yourself physically and mentally—sleeping properly, eating right, playing when you need it, and reflecting and meditating.
c) Be honest with yourself about who you are. Accept pain for what it is.

d) Accept your flaws. Find out the reasons why you believe the way you do.

e) Understand yourself and share yourself with the world.

f) Don't believe everything you think.

g) Decide what your purpose is and work toward that goal.

h) Be grateful.

i) Get out of your comfort-zone. Do something out of the ordinary!

j) People will try to pull you down, but you do not have to listen to them. Ignore the criticism!

k) Exercise!

l) Look at who you surround yourself with. Consider whether or not they are a negative or positive influence in your life. Let go of those who are negative.

m) Accept your emotions without judging them.

n) Get rid of these 5 toxic beliefs:

   a. The present is indicative of the future.

   b. Being vulnerable is dangerous.

   c. Being alone is a problem.

   d. Fitting in is a good thing.

   e. What everyone does to you is personal.

o) Do what you say you will do. Credibility is important!"
(Brown, 2019)

Types of Love

So let's go over each of these types of love one by one. Eros, of course, is erotic love. It is named after Eros, the Greek god of passion and sexual attraction (Burton, N., www.psychologytoday.com; www.greekmythology.com). Erotic love, then, is a physical love that may or may not have emotional ties to the other person. So many times a relationship is begun because two people are physically attracted to each other. Nothing else is there unless the couple gets to learn about each other. What I have found, however, is that many times we do not get to know each other before the physical relationship begins, so once the physical relationship begins, there is nothing to build the relationship on. There is no security. One can easily disengage from the relationship without being hurt emotionally.

Philia is affectionate love. This is usually love between friends. Love has formed because the two people have a personal and emotional bond. This brings up the question: Can a man and woman have philia without the relationship turning physical? Yes! But we have been told so much that it is not possible for a man and woman to have a nonsexual relationship that we tend to believe what the "majority" says!

Storge is familiar love (www.lonerwolf.com) and familial love (Burton, N., www.psychologytoday.com). It is a "natural form of affection that often flows between parents and their children, and children for their parents" (www.lonerwolf.com). So storge is not just familiar love, but familial love. Early relationships, such as best friends or those between a teacher and student, is often at this level of love. It is affection between two that have known each other for so long that they feel that they are family. I have one particular friend that I fully feel this way. She and I have known each other for so long that she is both my best friend and one that I feel is almost like a mother to me. She can tell me anything and I can tell her anything. Neither of us will judge each other.

Ludus is playful, teasing, physical, emotional, and what keeps a relationship going. Often this type of love is seen in relationships that are very new. It seems to be what is necessary at times to keep things moving, but is lost the longer we are emotionally involved with a person. The playfulness gives way to seriousness, and this is where many relationships go to die. It is once the seriousness comes in to play that a relationship will fall apart. But it does not have to be this way!

Another level of love is mania. It is not a healthy form of love by any means, because it is an obsessive love. According to www.lonerwolf.com, this form of love "occurs when there is an imbalance between eros and ludus. As you recall, eros is erotic and sexual in nature, and ludus is a playful love. "The person wants to love and be loved to find a sense of self value. Because of this, they can become possessive and jealous lovers, feeling as they desperately "need" their partners" (www.lonerwolf.com).

Pragma is an "enduring love" (www.lonerwolf.com), one that has stood the test of time. This is the type of love we all want but it is difficult to find. Maintaining is the key to having this type of love. It takes work from both involved, and requires compromise, patience, and tolerance in order to have an enduring love. Most young people do not have the ability to do this because they have not been taught the skills early on. How do we learn these skills? Learning how to compromise is something we need to be taught early on, but in our current society it is rare to learn. It is the skill of negotiating. We think of negotiating when we are at an auction, or buying a car, or even buying something at a garage sale. But it is more than this. It is trying to find a middle ground, a place where both people can agree on something, rather than disagree on everything. So often we see groups of people standing up for the rights of one particular group—prolife vs. prochoice, for example—but we have to remember that the group that is effected will need help considering both sides.

Philautia is self-love. This type of love is of extreme importance because without self-love we cannot truly give love. However, some people do take this to an extreme and only love themselves and are self-absorbed. This is not healthy. The self-absorbed person is not healthy in spirit or mentality.

Agape, as mentioned earlier, is a "perfect, unconditional, sacrificial, and pure" (www.thoughtco.com) love, but www.lonerwolf.com adds that it is a selfless love (also www.raptitude.com).

Another author, Robert Sternberg, suggests that there are three components to love: passion, intimacy, and commitment, and that the different combinations of these components are how the different forms of love come about (www.totescute.com, Definitions of Love Throughout the World). These components are very important in any type of love because without these components there are no real feelings.

What Love is Not

While we need to know what love is, we also need to know what love is not. Lonerwolf.com and psychologytoday.com both are good sources of information regarding the types of love. While love is difficult to fully define, it does not need to be confusing. On www.thebodyisnotanapology.com, Gittelman expresses what she believes is love, and what it is not. She expresses what love is not quite profoundly: American society in general, and the American woman specifically, has found that abuse has been normalized, and that it is almost expected, to be part of a loving relationship. This is untrue! Abuse of any sort—physical, emotional, mental, verbal, and sexual, among others—is NOT a sign of love!!! Stalking and obsession are NOT loving behaviors! When communication is difficult because you fear the person or what they will say, there is something wrong with the relationship. Love is not ownership, codependence, or dehumanizing. Love is not disrespectful. Love does not pressure you into acts you do not want to do, and finally, love does not gaslight or condescend you.

Love is not hateful. If another person loves you, they do not put themselves first. Or at least when they do put themselves first, they do not do it with the intention of hurting you. Love does not hurt! Being hit by a spouse, or being emotionally abused—any type of abuse for that matter—is not love! Love is thoughtful and caring. A person who loves can be "real" with someone, tell the person the things they need to hear, without hurting them. I have one friend who is like this. She can tell me something with a loving heart, and, even though what she says may sting a little, it is way better to hear the truth from her than to hear the truth in an ugly way from someone else. Even though she doesn't sugarcoat what she tells me, she does it in a way that makes me think about the situation.

Another author, Anapol ("What is Love, and What Isn't," www.psychologytoday.com), states many more things about what love is. "Love is a force of nature", and, like nature, we cannot control love "any more than we can command the moon and the stars and the wind and the rain to come and go according to our whims" (Anapol, www.psychologytoday.com). Love "is bigger than you are," "cannot be turned on as a reward or turned off as a punishment," "speaks out for justice and protests when harm is being done," and "cares what becomes of you" (Anapol, D., www.psychologytoday.com).

As Rabbi Wolpe stated earlier, love is an enacted emotion, and one where affection is felt for another. So actions such as hitting, sexually abusing, mental, verbal and emotional abuse are not signs of love, but rather signs that something is wrong in the person that is doing these things to the person that he or she claims to love. Abuse is not always perpetrated by the man, although many times we see this as a common occurrence just because men do not normally report abuse that is happening to them.

Biblical Study

Love can be felt in so many ways—a mother for her child, a love between husband and wife, a love between siblings or friends, and many others. A person can love an animal, a plant, or even music. But what does the Bible say about love? The most recognizable verse about love is found in 1 Corinthians 13:

If I speak in human and angelic tongues but do not love, I am a resounding gong or a clashing cymbal. And if I have the gift of prophecy and comprehend all mysteries and all knowledge; if I have all faith so as to move mountains, but do not love, I am nothing. If I give away everything I own and if I hand my body over so that I may boast but do not love, I gain nothing. Love is patient, love is kind. It is not jealous, [love] is not pompous, it is not inflated, it is not rude, it does not seek its own interests, it is not quick tempered, it does not brood over injury, it does not rejoice over wrongdoing but rejoices with the truth. It bears all things, believes all things, hopes all things, endures all things. Love never fails. If there are prophecies, they will be brought to nothing; if tongues, they will cease; if knowledge, it will be brought to nothing. For we know partially and we prophesy partially, but when the perfect comes, the partial will pass away. When I was a child, I used to talk as a child, think as a child, reason as a child; when I became a man, I put aside childish things. At present we see indistinctly, as in a mirror, but then face to face. At present I know partially, then I shall know fully, as I am fully known. So faith, hope, love remain, these three; but the greatest of these is love (1 Corinthians 13; NABRE).

"But to you who are listening I say: Love your enemies, do good to those who hate you, bless those who curse you, pray for those who mistreat you. If someone slaps you on one cheek, turn to them the other also. If someone takes your coat, do not withhold your shirt from them. Give to everyone who asks you, and if anyone takes what belongs to you, do not demand it back. Do to others as you would have them do to you" (Luke 6:27-33; NIV).

The love of the father is seen through the parable of the prodigal son (Luke 15:1-32). In it, the younger son tires of living the quiet life and wants to journey out into the world, to experience life. He asks his father for his share of inheritance and squanders it. He must then find work, and he works for a farmer feeding pigs. He comes to his senses when he realizes that his father's servants are fed better than he is, and he begins his journey home. He asks his father's forgiveness, and asks to be treated as one of his father's servants. His father sees his son in the distance, and runs to embrace his son. He has a feast for his returning son. The elder son is upset by all that his father is giving the younger son, but the father puts it into perspective when he says, "My son, the father said, you are always with me, and everything I have is yours. But we had to celebrate and be glad, because this brother of yours was dead and is alive again; he was lost and is found" (Luke 15:31-32). This is what love is all about!

"Love must be sincere. Hate what is evil; cling to what is good. Be devoted to one another in love. Honor one another above yourselves. Never be lacking in zeal, but keep your spiritual fervor, serving the Lord. Be joyful in hope, patient in affliction, faithful in prayer. Share with the Lord's people who are in need. Practice hospitality. Bless those who persecute you; bless and do not curse. Rejoice with those who rejoice; mourn with those who mourn. Live in harmony with one another. Do not be proud, but be willing to associate with people of low position. Do not be conceited. Do not repay evil with evil. Be careful to do what is right in the eyes of everyone. If it is possible, as far as it depends on you, live at peace with everyone. Do not take revenge, my dear friends, but leave room for God's wrath, for it is written: "It is mine to avenge; I will repay," says the Lord. On the contrary: "If your enemy is hungry, feed him; if he is thirsty, give him something to drink. In doing this, you will heap burning coals on his head." Do not be overcome by evil, but overcome evil with good (Romans 12:9-21; NIV). St. Paul is very descriptive on what love is all about, that we are to love our neighbor at all times, even if our neighbor is an enemy.

Things to Think About

To love and feel loved are both wonderful feelings! We feel important to others when we are loved. How can we make others feel important, to feel loved? In showing others that they are important to us, we are sharing our values. What do you value about the person? Share with the person what you see in them that you value. Show the person that they are important to you. Thanking them for the good things you see in them will make the person start thinking about the things they value in others.

Think about the ways you express emotion toward others, and how others express toward you. Do you express through anger and frustration, or hitting? Does someone do this to you? Consider how often these expressions occur. Is it something that has happened so frequently that it is habitual? Or is it something that occurs rarely? How does the relationship make you feel? Do you need to get out of this relationship? Consider how the person makes you feel. Really think about it! Maybe the relationship is not right for you.

Rejection

"Rejection can be defined as the act of pushing someone or something away" (www.goodtherapy.org). When rejection happens to us it can be very painful, as often we have no idea why we are being rejected, or we feel that we should be accepted just as we are. Depending on how often it is done, the rejection can have short-term and long-term consequences. If the rejection only happens on occasion, such as a parent telling a child that they cannot have a snack before dinner, the child may be hurt for a short while but understands because he or she knows the rules about snacks before dinner. However, long-term rejection, which consistently and repeatedly happens to someone, can have serious psychological consequences both in school and in personal relationships with classmates or work relationships (www.goodtherapy.org). Mental illnesses such as depression and anxiety, or chronic fear of rejection, can be worsened by the way that the rejected person responds to the rejection. Depression is frequently seen in females who have been rejected. Bullying is seen as a form of rejection that is combined with being ostracized and is frequently seen in males who are depressed, although females sometimes do bullying as well.

Feeling rejected by someone is one of the most unpleasant feelings. We ask ourselves why we are being rejected, and many times we will never get the answer. There are so many reasons a person is rejected! Garcy (2019) suggests that when you feel rejected you need to work to "reclaim your power over your happiness, rather than putting it into the hands of another person [because] you cannot control the other person's choices or opinions"

For the depressed person, to be socially accepted only gives temporary relief (Wood, 2018, www.psychcentral.com). Why would the relief only be temporary? Well, the depressed individual has no real way to regulate their emotions. It seems that the opioid system, a system that is involved in expression of emotion, may be responsible (Wood, 2018). Physical pain and depression are expressed in similar ways because physical and mental pain involve the same brain regions (Staple, www.sciencefocus.com; Eisenberger and Lieberman, 2004, 1). This is obviously an evolutionary adaptation. Physical pain is defined as the "unpleasant sensory and emotional experience associated with actual or potential tissue damage," while social pain is defined as the "distressing experience arising from the perception of actual or potential psychological distance from close others or a social group" (Eisenberger and Lieberman, 2004, 1).

Rejection can come about for superficial reasons, like not liking the way a person looks, or for more substantial reasons, such as your political or religious views do not match with another person's views. Even financial or psychological reasons could be reasons for rejection. "Those who have difficulty trusting are usually those who have been rejected or abused" (Glasser, Choice Theory, 49). Leary (2015) suggests that rejection was a development of survival, that those who were rejected were less likely to survive in the early years of evolution, and that those who were accepted were more likely to survive in the world in which they lived, similar in thought to Darwin's theory that those who survived were more capable of survival (436).

The fear of rejection is almost always worse than the rejection itself. How can we conquer this fear realistically? Harvey Mackay (2011, 6 Ways to Conquer the Fear of Rejection, www.inc.com) offers several guidelines that are helpful not just for businesses, but also for people on an individual level. First, we must "dissect thoughts under the microscope." If we are having negative thoughts, we must change it into positive thinking! Next, we must "identify realistic fears," see if there are realistic fears within us that are making the situation unbearable. Third, we must "focus on the moment," remember that once we are past the moment that we can move to the next opportunity. Next, we must be more assertive, express what we need and say no to requests where we genuinely cannot help. We must then analyze the failure, figure out why we failed at the given task, whether or not it is in an attempt to build a new friendship or to get past the fear of going on an outing. Finally, don't rationalize away the hurt by saying "it was bound to happen" or "it was meant to be." Being defined by others and accepting that as truth is where many of us falter. We are who we believe we are! Everything worth having is worth the effort!

Interpersonal rejection sensitivity, as defined by Hall (2013, blogs.psychcentral.com), is a "hyper-alertness to the social reactions of others" (Hall, 2013, www.psychcentral.com). The rejection sensitive person usually is anxious and expects rejection, but then they overreact to the rejection. Misinterpretation of what the other person means is extremely common in the rejection sensitive person. Those who are not emotionally sensitive are often confused and do not know why the sensitive person is reacting the way they are. The sensitive person understands this as rejection, and feels as if they are unacceptable to others. The depression becomes deeper, and the emotionally sensitive person becomes angry, feels like a failure, so even if the other person is accepting of them, the emotionally sensitive person is only temporarily relieved.

If you are emotionally sensitive, there are several things to do to help you cope with this sensitivity:

a) Be aware of how rejection sensitivity affects you.

b) Pause before you react. Keep calm before responding to the person you believe has rejected you.

c) Consider reasons for the other person's behavior.

d) CALMLY ask the person about their intention.

e) Consider the facts of the other person's life. Are they a single parent of several small children? Do they have a stressful job?

f) Participate fully in events and activities.

(Hall, Karyn, 2013; blogs.psychcentral.com/emotionally-sensitive/2013/05/rejection-sensitivity)

How do we cope with rejection of someone that we truly liked as a person? How can we make the best of rejection, for whatever reason? These are two very important questions to be answered here. I had been rejected by someone who had been a good friend for several months. How did I deal with it? First off, the person told me why he was rejecting me. He and I had only been friends, but the rejection was painful. He had helped me through a particularly difficult situation. I understood why he was rejecting me, but I also needed a good friend, and I had felt that he was a good friend, someone I could talk to about anything. So I accepted his rejection and just let him be. A few days ago, after not speaking to each other for several months, he messaged me and we got caught up on what had been happening over the last several months. I feel lucky to have a friendship recovering, but this does not always happen.

Coping with rejection, according to www.goodtherapy.org, is a multi-step process. We must "acknowledge the event and accept that it was painful." We must then express our feelings out loud (to ourselves or to someone else). We must then stop dwelling on the event, although this can be very difficult for a lot of people. We must be objective about the rejection and stop blaming ourselves and avoid negative thoughts. Reaching out to family and friends who are supportive can help the pain lessen, and doing something active, such as exercising, can help relieve the pain as well (www.goodtherapy.org).

Responses to rejection include hurt feelings, jealousy, loneliness and homesickness, guilt and shame, social anxiety and embarrassment, sadness and anger (Leary, 437-439), mental illnesses such as depression and anxiety, and coping mechanisms such as eating disorders and self-harming behaviors (www.goodtherapy.org). One of the most common forms of rejection that many of us experience is the rejection of a romantic partner, otherwise known as hurt feelings. The rejected person is perceived to have a low relational value, their importance no longer exists in the eyes of the other person. The common phrase, "It's not you, it's me," is used frequently in rejecting a person. Interestingly, it is not the right phrase to use. We should be using the phrase, "It's because of both of us. I don't feel the same way about you that you do for me." But how many times do we take the blame solely for ourselves? Almost all the time!

Sylvia DeMichiel (2018) suggests four ways to handle rejection when you are depressed or anxious:

a) "Allow yourself to feel whatever you need to feel."
b) "Do your best not to jump to the worst possible conclusion."
c) "Do your best to believe there is something better waiting for you."
d) "Never give up" (DeMichiel, 2018).

Building up one's resilience—the way the person responds or reacts to the rejection—is of utmost importance. How we do that is by developing a strong support system that consists of those who care about us. It can include family, friends, a pastor, or even a counselor or psychotherapist. By addressing issues such as chronic rejection, or our fears and insecurities, and the reasons why we feel the way we do, even going so far back as early childhood, we can learn to deal with rejection in a more effective way.

Jealousy occurs when people "believe that another person values his or her relationship with them less than they desire because of the presence or intrusion of a third party" (Leary, 437). It could be jealousy over a sibling getting more attention than others in a family unit, or jealousy over a new person getting more attention from a close friend.

Another form of rejection is at the voting booth. We accept one person's political opinion over another, thereby rejecting another person or persons for a particular political office. Many times we will watch on television the political concession of one candidate to another because the person did not win. How does the loser make the best of this situation? Most likely by getting back into the seat and figuring out another way to win the next time.

Loneliness and homesickness are other ways we respond to rejection. "People experience loneliness and homesickness when they believe that people who greatly value their relationship are not available for social interaction and support" (Leary, 437-438). Just this year I suffered from a large amount of loneliness because of a situation I was in. I felt that no one cared about me except for 2 or 3 people. Between my children moving to a city two hours away, and then being isolated from all those that I loved because I was in jail, I suffered a great amount of loneliness. Fortunately there were several people that helped keep me upbeat through their writing letters and visiting me. Otherwise I could not have gotten through the struggles that I had this year.

Guilt and shame are often tied to our feelings of rejection. We feel guilt for doing certain things, or shame that we are unable to do what we want to do, so we isolate ourselves. Guilt is felt because we have done something bad, and shame is felt when we feel we are a bad person. I might feel guilty because I didn't finish my homework, but I might feel shame because I was being bad by not doing my homework.

Social anxiety and embarrassment are in a completely different ballpark than the others because social anxiety is a psychological disorder that is usually brought on by embarrassment (Leary, 438-439). Social anxiety, according to the DSM-5, is when the individual is "fearful or anxious about or avoidant of social interactions and situations that involve the possibility of being scrutinized. These include social interactions such as meeting unfamiliar people, situations in which the individual may be observed eating or drinking, and situations in which the individual performs in front of others. The cognitive ideation is of being negatively evaluated by others, by being embarrassed, humiliated, or rejected, or offending others" (APA, 190).

Sadness and anger are emotions that are brought on by other factors. Sadness comes about because of a "perceived loss" (Leary,439), and anger occurs "when people perceive that another agent (usually, but not always a person) has unjustifiably behaved in an undesired fashion that threatens their desires or well-being"

(Leary, 439). The anger could be at oneself, or it could be toward another person.

 But what if a person's rejection of something is because of financial reasons? If you have been rejected by someone because of a financial issue, you are better off without the person, but what if you feel ashamed because you can no longer be a part of an organization that you enjoy being a member of? Say you have been a member of an organization for a number of years, and you have always tried to be participant in the different activities that the organization has hosted. All of a sudden, though, you are hit with some major expenses and can no longer participate in the once loved group. You quit going to the meetings and a member wonders why, so they come and ask about why you quit going. They know that you enjoyed being a member, and that it was always a meaningful part of the week for you. So they ask you why you quit going. You break down and tell them why—that you can't afford to be a member anymore, that you have certain things you must do each month, and after all these expenses, you can no longer afford to do the things you once did. The member understands, and when they walk away they go to the other members of the group and discuss the dilemma. As a result you are able to continue on with being a member because someone else has taken on the financial responsibility for you because they know that you are contributing member and your contribution to the group means more than any financial contribution that you would be making. By understanding the rejection and the reasons why you had rejected the group, the other group members were able to help you cope with the things you had to deal with. Being accepted into the group as a new member was great, but knowing that you are a valued member of the group makes you feel even better because of the other contributions that you make to the group. By talking it out with other members you are able to continue on as a member, even if financially you cannot help the group. The members have found other ways for you to contribute.

Fear of rejection can look like many things. Not showing who you truly are (being phony), people-pleasers, lacking confidence, being passive-aggressive, and the physical attributes such as sweating, fidgeting, avoiding eye contact are common ways that people show their fears (Fritscher, 2018).

Rejection can look like many things as well. For example, silent treatment, anger or rage, and even being unfriended or unfollowed on social media are all forms of rejection, as well as the common rejection letter we get from businesses and schools. But how can we use rejection to help us to become better people? First off, don't take the rejection to heart (Ahuja, www.entrepreneur.com). Taking it personally just makes you depressed. If you take it personally, the failure and rejection can really bring you down, and this is not how you need to be when you are rejected. Second, you need to pick yourself up, dust yourself off, and do some positive self-talk (Ahuja, www.entrepreneur.com; Scott (2018), www.verywellmind.com).

Dealing with Rejection

Amy Morin (2015) (*5 Ways Mentally Strong People Deal With Rejection*, www.inc.com) suggests five ways that mentally strong people deal with rejection. Included are: a) Acknowledge their emotions; b) View rejection as evidence they're pushing the limits; c) Treat themselves with compassion; d) Refuse to let rejection define them; and e) Learn from rejection. These are all very important factors! If we do not do these things, the rejection can lead us down the black hole of depression, which is very difficult to get out of. However, I would like to add that using positive self-talk is very important to do as well, because how we talk to ourselves shows us how we deal with difficulties. If we can deal with rejection in a positive manner, then we can lead ourselves out of the black hole.

Pamela D. Garcy (2019) found that while getting over a personal rejection can be difficult, there are ways to productively cope with the rejection, and even suggested several benefits (Yes, benefits!) to being rejected! In order to get into the right train of thought, you must first breathe, settle, and focus. The benefits of rejection include:

a) You can learn to remember your own strengths and good qualities, leading to a better self-relationship.

b) You can return to your self-care routine, leading you to experience improved mental and physical health.

c) You can practice creativity in other life areas, leading you to remember your own resilience and other passionate interests.

d) You can develop clarity through remembering the boundaries of the situation; let yourself off the hook a little!

e) You can improve your social skills, leading you to have greater social awareness and grace.

f) You can learn to be happy, despite the rejection, teaching yourself that your emotional well-being rests in your hands.

g) You can learn to see this as an opening instead of a closing.

h) You can release your need to prove yourself and/or be right.

i) You can practice being positive in the midst of adversity, developing a more sturdy sense of self (Garcy, 2019).

Positive self-talk is a coping skill that we can easily learn and adapt to our needs. It includes things such as visualization, using positive words in thoughts and talking, and using positive affirmations (Ahuja, www.enterpreneur.com, *6 ways to Overcome Rejections*). How does positive self-talk work? It gives you a way to refocus on what you really need to focus on. I'll use myself as an example. I've been told many times that there was no way to achieve my dreams, no way to get past the limits that others put on me. I sustained a traumatic brain injury when I was 2 ½ years old. The doctors had no idea what I might be able to do, and so they gave my parents no real idea of what they thought I might be capable of. So my parents did what any good parents would do. They took me home after he hospital stay and worked with me daily on learning the things they knew I needed to know. When I was 4 years old they had me go to a special school for children with difficulty learning, so that I wouldn't be so far behind when I began regular school the following year. Although I did learn a bit slower than my classmates, I did graduate from high school on time. But it wasn't until I was in 11th grade that I began practicing positive self-talk, attempting to improve academically so that I could go further in life. At that time I realized that I would be going to college soon, and I needed to do better in my grades. By using positive self-talk and working harder than ever, I was able to raise my grades almost an entire grade! I was the same way in college. I had to do a lot of positive self-talk just to make certain I kept going, kept motivating myself by saying that no one believed I would ever get this far! I used the encouragement of others, and the positive self-talk, as a motivator in my academic life. Then I went to graduate school many years later, and I had four people standing behind me (my children and my spouse), cheering me on the whole way! Positive self-talk can work you through rejection as well! Other ways to deal with rejection are to love and value yourself, to visualize success, and to trust the universe (Ahuja, *6 ways to Overcome Rejections,* www.enterpreneur.com).

Biblical Study

Throughout life there are times when we all feel rejected, lonely, heartbroken, and downright depressed. However, in praying we can feel connected to God. Upon reading the following passages, I have frequently felt that someone is always there, guiding me on my way, and that God will be here with me even if humans are not.

What does the Bible say about rejection? "But the Lord said to Samuel, 'Do not consider his appearance or his height, for I have rejected him. The Lord does not look at the things people look at. People look at the outward appearance, but the Lord looks at the heart'" (1 Samuel 16:7; NIV). It hurts when we are rejected, but we have to remember that a rejection from one person may bring the acceptance by another.

"The Lord is close to the brokenhearted and saves those who are crushed in spirit" (Psalms 34:18; NIV). When we feel rejected or depressed because of situations beyond our control, we need to pray. By allowing our focus to be released from our mind and heart, we can look at the difficulty more clearly.

"Commit your way to the Lord; trust in him and he will do this: He will make your righteous reward shine like the dawn, your vindication like the noonday sun. Be still before the Lord and wait patiently for him; do not fret when people succeed in their ways, when they carry out their wicked schemes" (Psalms 37:5-7; NIV).

Things to Think About

Rejection is one of the worse things to experience because it brings about so many negative feelings. While rejection can hurt, we can also get through rejection by utilizing positive self-talk, a way to help ourselves cope with the feelings we have when we feel rejection. Positive self-talk can work in other situations as well, such as when you are struggling with a problem that doesn't seem solvable. Other ways to deal with rejection are to be creative, taking care of yourself, and remember where your strengths lie. Taking control of your emotional well-being is extremely important, as it teaches you about how you want to be treated, as well as helping you to set boundaries as well.

PART II

Emotional Reactions

Emotions can be overwhelming when a relationship begins or ends. The following chapters are many of the emotions that can occur at any stage of a relationship, and emotions that you can have with family, friends, associates, lovers, significant others, or spouse— any type of relationship. You may even feel these types of feelings if you have a relationship with God or any other religious entity. Each type of relationship is part of our journey in life. As with the previous section, there is a section that includes some Biblical passages that relate to the chapter topic. I hope that you get as much out of that section as you do for the other parts of each chapter as well.

Happiness

Happiness is mostly experienced because of the love we receive from others. However, happiness can also occur because we choose NOT to be affected by others in our life. Toxic people can bring us down in a heartbeat, but only if you allow them to do so.

What exactly is happiness? While we have whole books related to different emotional disorders (what we deem negative topics), it is not common for happiness (a positive topic) to be researched. To be happy means you feel or show pleasure or contentment (Ackerman, www.positivepsychology.com, 2019). That means that happiness is a state of being, not a trait.

Happiness in positive psychology has been approached in several ways:

a) Happiness as a global assessment of life and all its facets

b) Happiness as a recollection of past emotional experiences

c) Happiness as an aggregation of multiple emotional reactions across time

d) Self-happiness "refers to a sense of happiness or satisfaction with one's self…. you are pleased with yourself and your choices and with the person that you are" (Ackerman, 2019, www.positivpsychology.com)

Purpose

Most people think things such as: I'll be happy when I have someone in my life. I'll be happy when I have a job. I'll be happy when my children are out of the house. But happiness does not come from a situation. It comes from having a purpose and fulfillment. What do I need to do in order to be fulfilled? What is my purpose? Why am I going through this challenge right now? For many years all I knew was that my purpose was to help others. I had to figure out, through thought and prayer, how best I could fulfill this purpose. To find a purpose you must first find something that you enjoy doing. By doing what you enjoy, you are able to focus on what your reality, your life, is leading you to do. Purpose gives a reason for being. My purpose is to help others in their lives.

How do you find your purpose? Look at the things that bring you meaning, that bring you happiness. For the last few years my life slowly went downhill. Financially I was having difficulties, which brought added stress, and I was having difficulty taking care of my three children. I felt meaning by having them with me. But in December 2017 I had a situation come up that made it difficult to care for my children. My hours at work had been decreased a lot. A sister of mine and her husband offered to take all three boys with them to live. So they moved two hours away. My mental health declined because I felt like I had no purpose anymore.

Depression and anxiety were very high. Then I got arrested and spent 4 months in jail. After I got out of jail, I found it difficult to find work right away. I thought that maybe I would be able to find a job right away, and that I would be able to save up some money so that the boys could move back in with me that same year. But life sometimes throws you overboard into a stormy sea. I found work, but then I was fired several months later. Then I couldn't find work again, no matter how hard I tried. I felt that I had no purpose. Having a job would give me purpose. But very few people will hire someone who has been arrested. Nothing was going right. Then I found a job that I enjoyed. I found meaning. I found that I was happier. By getting work I am able to focus more on the things I need to do to get done so that I can eventually get my family relationships and my life back on track.

Toxic People

What are toxic people? A toxic person is "anyone who is abusive, unsupportive, or unhealthy emotionally—someone who basically brings you down more than up" (Langslet, K., 3 Signs a Toxic Person is Manipulating You... www.greatist.com). A toxic person will give you a purpose, but that purpose is usually to make him or her happy, not you. And you can never do enough for the toxic person. You are always trying to make them happy and never managing to reach that goal.

According to Abigail Brenner (Psychology Today, 2016), there are eight traits of toxic people. They are:

a) They are manipulative
b) They are judgmental.
c) They take no responsibility for their own feelings. Rather, their feelings are projected onto you.
d) They don't apologize.
e) They are inconsistent.
f) They make you prove yourself to them.
g) They make you defend yourself.
h) They are not caring, supportive, or interested in what's important to you.

Brenner also states to "weigh the pros (if there are any) and the cons, make a decision to limit your time with this person or end the relationship—and don't look back" (Brenner, A., 8 Things the Most Toxic People. . ., www.psychologytoday.com; Brown, L., 15 Common Traits of Toxic People; www.ideapod.com). In addition to the previous traits, Brown (2017) adds: They can't listen to you because they are thinking about themselves and how they can get something out of it; they are not supportive of your wants and needs; they interrupt a lot and find the negative in everything they do and say; they never admit defeat; they will never go out of their way for you; are attention seekers; they won't go out of their way to help you; and they are mean (Brown, L., June 17, 2017, 15

Common Traits of Toxic People; www.ideapod.com). The thing about toxic people is you cannot control how they act toward you, but you can control how you react to them. Take control of your life!

<u>Ways to Let Go of Toxicity and Bring in Happiness</u>

May Peterson (July 2, 2019) gave several ways to let go of a toxic relationship:

a) Don't look back. Looking back stops the healing process.

b) Accept that it's going to be pretty lonely at first.

c) Give yourself a break. Forgive yourself, grieve the loss, and move on.

d) Expect opposition. Opposition always comes against positive change.

e) Don't think you're the only one. And don't be too proud to ask for help.

f) Refuse to be negative! Think and talk about rebuilding and growth. Your thoughts and words affect your heart, so keep them positive!

g) Pray! Apply prayer directly to your pain each day. Ask God to heal your wounds, cleanse your attitude, and rebuild your future. **Pray specific to your needs! (It is not selfish to pray for yourself!!!)**

h) Evaluate what you have learned throughout the previous relationship, and what you need and want in the future.

i) Trust God to heal you.

j) Invest in your soul. Go to church. Read the Bible and other spiritual books.

(Peterson, May (July2, 2019). 10 Ways to Let Go of a Toxic Relationship.)

Biblical Study

"My command is this: Love each other as I have loved you. Greater love has no one than this: to lay down one's life for one's friends (John 15:12-13; NIV).

"And when you pray, do not be like the hypocrites, for they love to pray standing in the synagogues and on the street corners to be seen by others. Truly I tell you, they have received their reward in full. But when you pray, go into your room, close the door and pray to your Father, who is unseen. Then your Father, who sees what is done in secret, will reward you. And when you pray, do not keep on babbling like pagans, for they think they will be heard because of their many words. Do not be like them, for your Father knows what you need before you ask him" (Matthew 6:5-8; NIV).

Things to Think About

Take out a piece of paper and write down all the things you are thankful for, that bring you happiness. Tack it up on the wall where you will look at it every day. Now think about and write down, on a separate piece of paper, the things that bring you sadness. Take this piece of paper, crumble it up, and throw it away. By crumbling it up and letting it go, and focusing on the things that make you happy, you can refocus your thoughts and focus on the happiness in your life. What do you have to be happy for?

Stress

Stress is the result of feeling that you are out of control of a situation. It can result in depression or anxiety, mainly because of the way that you cope with the given situation. According to Pegues (2007), "Stress is our biological response to the pressures of life. The pressures do not necessarily have to be negative to have a negative impact on our bodies, nor must they be the things that are the obvious" (13; Handly and Neff, 30). We oftentimes can get overwhelmed by the stressors in our lives because it is too much for us to cope with mentally, physically, or emotionally.

Having high expectations of yourself and others is one way to add undue stress to your life. Although high expectations can give you something to work toward, in the end the stress that it gives you will have an impact on your physical and mental health. For example, if you expect yourself to be able to work ten hour days in addition to making dinner, keeping the house immaculate, and taking care of other responsibilities, you will likely find yourself burned out because you have too many things to do. Having realistic expectations, such as working and making dinner, and having someone else in the house to take care of the other responsibilities would be better. Your spouse, for example, can take care of the trash and the dishes, while one of your children can dry the dishes and put them away.

Limit the time you spend with those who bring you stress. This could be a family member, an associate from work, or even a member of an organization in which you are involved. If you notice that someone you know is causing you a great amount of stress, first speak with the person. Find out what is going on. They may not even be aware of the stress that they have added to your life. If this does not alleviate the situation, then stop associating with them. If you cannot stop associating with the person, then limit the amount of time you spend with them, like an hour a week, if possible. If your job is causing an undue amount of stress, consider getting a different, less stressful job. If your personal life is causing the stress, sit down and decide what areas of your life are essential and don't worry about the nonessential areas. Pegues (2007) poses several questions for you to consider when dealing with stress-inducing people:

a) "Will this situation produce patience in me if I endure it rather than run away?

b) Why does this person's action stress me? Is it because she is mirroring my behavior?

c) Why am I choosing to continue to interact with her" (Pegues, 93)?

Anger

An undue amount of stress can bring anger into the picture. Anger turned outward is rage, and anger turned inward is grief. Anger can be very destructive if not handled in an appropriate manner. Some turn to mind-altering drugs (prescription, alcohol, or illegal drug use). Others learn coping skills, such as meditation, yoga, journaling, or projects that are useful (e.g. woodworking or mechanical work).

Firestone (www.psychalive.org/simple-truth-anger) found that "suppressing angry feelings inevitably has destructive consequences" and suggested that there are four major effects of bypassing the feeling of angry emotions:

a) Developing psychosomatic symptoms, and play a part in the development of physical illnesses such as headaches, hypertension, cardiovascular disease, and cancer.

b) Turning the anger against oneself, causes the person to become self-critical and self-hating. This brings to mind such problems as self-harm, such as cutting, and eating disorders.

c) Projecting anger outward onto others in methods and reacting to the perceived enemies with counter-aggression or paranoia.

d) Acting out hostile or negative behaviors because they cannot tolerate angry emotions. They are hurtful and abusive toward themselves and others and usually act against their best interests. Stifling their anger "causes them to act in a passive-aggressive manner or by using withholding behaviors, such as being forgetful, being habitually late, procrastinating and otherwise provoking others.... They tend to justify the reasons for their anger, which leads to feeling misunderstood, victimized, righteously indignant or morally wronged"

(Firestone, www.psychalive.org/simple-truth-anger).

McLeod (2010, www.mcleodandmore.com/2010/07/19/angervdepression) states that "Depression is often anger turned inward, and anger is often depression turned outward." She gives the following advice: "Give yourself permission to experience the real emotion. If you're angry, just admit it. And if you're sad, give yourself permission to sit with it. The quicker you acknowledge the real emotion, the better chance you'll have of working through it."

Ways to Cope with Stress

What are some ways to cope with stress? First, we need to slow down, focus on the really important parts of the situation. For most people, finances are at the top of the list of stressors. You need food, clothing, and shelter, but you also have a car payment, cell phone, cable or satellite TV, tithing, and expenses regarding your children. You have no idea how you are going to make it. You feel completely overwhelmed! Sit down, breathe slowly, and focus on what the absolute necessities are.

What are the necessities? Food, clothing, and shelter are the most important because they are necessary to survive. Consider the things that a homeless person has to have in order to survive. They do without everything but the clothes on their back. Food may be scarce, and shelter is certainly wanted but if they have no job, shelter will be difficult to come by, especially if they live in a small town. Homeless shelters are very rarely in small towns, and shelters usually have an overabundance of occupants in cities. Medication may be another of their needs, but because they lack shelter, the medication is an expense they cannot take care of. If you think about the basic needs and take care of those first, then you can look at your other expenses and break them down into needs and wants. Those that are wants can only be considered when the needs are taken care of.

Another way to help yourself not have as much stress is to neaten up your work area. Is it usually a mess? Take some time to tidy the area up so that your mind and your work space is not cluttered. I don't know about you, but it helps me to have an organized work space so that I can think more clearly.

Physical exercise and meditation are also good ways to lessen the load that stress puts on you. How does physical exercise help? "When your brain senses a threat or danger, it quickly releases hormones carrying an urgent message via the bloodstream to the adrenal glands (which sit atop the kidneys) .... The adrenal glands produce excess stress chemicals, cortisol and adrenaline, and rushes them into the bloodstream, where they get delivered to various parts of the body via nerve fibers. The body responds with increased strength, raised blood pressure, and other assistance needed to resist or run" (Pegues, 30). Other ways to release the tension in your body include taking a deep breath, squeezing an anti-stress ball, singing, or giving yourself a massage (Pegues, 98-100).

Laughter, it is claimed, is one of the best medicines to treat mental illness and stress (www.vantagepointrecovery.com/laughter-mental-health). Even the magazine *Readers Digest* has a column named Laughter: The Best Medicine. How can laughter be good for us?

a) It is hard to feel negative emotions while laughing.

b) Stress is reduced when laughing.

c) Energy increases while laughing.

d) Helps engage others socially, which allows you to be less overwhelmed and more spontaneous and confident.

e) Releases endorphins.

f) Eases anxiety.

g) Improves overall mood and functioning.

(www.vantagepointrecovery.com/laughter-mental-health)

Laughter is considered an emotional medicine because it can reduce stress, anger, and loneliness (www.vantagepointrecovery.com/laughter-mental-health).

There are many physical benefits to laughter, including the release of endorphins in the brain which in turn tells us to be happy, the stress hormone cortisol is reduced, more oxygen circulates in the body, and muscles are exercised (www.vantagepointrecovery.com/laughter-mental-health).

Dopamine is necessary in order for a fear to be eliminated. When dopamine neurons are active, fear and anxiety do not occur (Davies, J., www.lifeadvancer.com). There are several ways to increase dopamine function in your brain. Diet, supplements, getting sunshine, getting a regular massage, and taking a cold shower are all ways to increase dopamine functioning (Davies, J., www.lifeadvancer.com). Getting a massage reduces tension and stress, decreases the stress hormone cortisol by 31%, and increases dopamine by an average of 30%. Taking an ice-cold shower has even better results, raising dopamine levels by 250% and increases our endorphins (Davies, J., www.lifeadvancer.com).

Diet is very important. By increasing your intake of tyrosine, which is found in meat such as chicken, turkey, and roast beef, seafood (salmon and fish), dairy products (milk, cottage cheese, yogurt, parmesan cheese, swiss cheese, and provolone cheese), ripe bananas and watermelon, beans, soy products, and green tea, you will be aiding your body in its ability to use dopamine. Decreasing your sugar intake is also essential. By eating yogurt, sauerkraut, pickles, dark chocolate, and olives (among others), as well as drinking apple cider vinegar, the toxins in your gut will be reduced. Many people take supplements. Supplements that help with the functioning of dopamine include Dopa Mucuna, L-theanine, Ginkgo Biloba, Rhodiola, and Curcumin (Davies, J.).

Socializing with positive, happy people helps us to become more positive, bringing down stress, which makes it less likely for depression, fear, and anxiety to exist. Stress levels go down, and as the stress levels go down, so do anxiety, depression, and fear. Dopamine increases and becomes more active. Even smiling has been shown to help with the production of dopamine—and it doesn't have to be a real smile either, although I would imagine a real smile would increase dopamine levels greater than a fake smile.

Another possible way to bring down stress levels is through prayer or talking to a friend. By allowing another person into your circle and opening up about what is going on in your life that is so stressful, you are allowing someone else in to help.

Biblical Study

"Wait for the Lord; be strong and take heart and wait for the Lord" (Psalms 27:14; NIV).

"The Lord is good to those whose hope is in him, to the one who seeks him. It is good to wait quietly for the salvation of the Lord" (Lamentations 3:25-26; NIV).

"The end of a matter is better than its beginning, and patience is better than pride. Do not be quickly provoked in your spirit, for anger resides in the lap of fools" (Ecclesiastes 7:8-9; NIV).

"My dear brothers and sisters, take note of this: Everyone should be quick to listen, slow to speak and slow to become angry, because human anger does not produce the righteousness that God desires" (James 1:19-20; NIV).

"Fools give full vent to their rage, but the wise bring calm in the end" (Proverbs 29:11; NIV).

Things to Think About

Becoming overwhelmed by a stressful situation is common to most people. Stress can bring about anger and depression as well as anxiety. What is there that you can do to become less stressed? Is there a friend that you can turn to when you are stressed, someone that can help you to focus what is most important? How about making a list of your responsibilities and then prioritize them? Make it a habit to think first before reacting so that the stress does not inflate into worse problems, such as anger and depression.

Grief

Grief is defined as an intense sadness that is often associated with death. However, it does not have to be the physical death of someone that brings about grief. It can be a death of a relationship, or the death of a project, that brings about grief. According to William C. Shiel Jr. (Medical Definition of Grief; www.medicinenet.com) , the medical definition of grief is: "The normal process of reacting to a loss. The loss may be physical (such as a death), social (such as divorce), or occupational (such as a job). Emotional reactions of grief can include anger, guilt, anxiety, sadness, and despair. Physical reactions of grief can include sleeping problems, changes in appetite, physical problems, or illness" (www.medicinenet.com). There can be other forms of grief, such as anticipatory grief or complicated grief, but the above definition is a good general definition of what grief is and the emotional and physical responses that can occur.

Grief is frequently seen as a temporary sadness with a time of adjustment to the new situation. However, if the grief seems to carry on for an extended period of time, treatment such as counseling should be looked into so that new coping skills are learned.

Stages of Grief

According to Elizabeth Kubler-Ross, there are five stages of grief. They are:

a) Denial

b) Anger

c) Bargaining

d) Depression

e) Acceptance

These stages can go in any order. Usually, however, denial is the first stage.

The stage of denial is also where we feel shock. "If you receive news on the death of a loved one, perhaps you cling to a false hope that they identified the wrong person.. In the denial stage, you are not living in 'actual reality,' rather you are living in a 'preferable' reality" (Gregory, 2019; www.psycom.net).

Anger occurs when you are upset with the other person, or upset about the situation. It could be because they abandoned you and the friendship you had, or because you are mad that someone died. It could be a number of reasons.

Bargaining primarily occurs after a diagnosis, but can occur because you are trying to salvage a relationship of some sort.

Trying to talk it out, for example, might be seen as a form of bargaining because there would be some sort of compromise in order to keep a friendship or romantic relationship intact.

Depression happens when one realizes that the person is really gone from their lives, whether through physical death, moving away, breaking up, or divorce. The person realizes that they were dependent on someone or something because the loss is both physical and mental.

Acceptance finally occurs as the person finally realizes that even though they do not like what happened, they can deal with the situation in a productive manner. Some people, however, never get to the acceptance stage. It really depends on how they have dealt with the situation from early on.

Treatment for Grief

Treatment for grief is often counseling or at least opening up to a friend or other confidant, such as a priest or minister. "When one is in trouble," and grief is considered a trouble, Sheen (1955) said that "one should never go for advice to one who never says prayers or who has not passed through suffering" (Sheen, 110). This makes a lot of sense for most people. Who would go to someone for counseling who has not gone through a similar experience? Who would go to someone who doesn't pray at least for guidance in helping those that he or she helps? I would have difficulty going to someone who did not pray, or to one who has not gone through a similar experience. Wouldn't you?

Oftentimes the counseling occurs one-on-one, such as a client and therapist setting, but many times the grieving person will go to group therapy since the people within the group will have gone through similar issues. Someone who is alone for the first time in many years, however, may have difficulty in opening up to a group of people, no matter the similarities in their lives.

Biblical Passages

One of the books of the Bible that I have always found comforting is the book of Psalms. Passages related to depression, grief, and anxiety, among other topics, have always been found to be beneficial to my heart in times of need. Here are some passages, not just from Psalms, but from other parts of the Bible as well, that have helped me in times of sorrow and grief.

Psalm 34:18 The Lord is close to the brokenhearted and saves those who are crushed in spirit.

Psalm 147:3 He heals the brokenhearted and binds up their wounds.

Psalm 55:22 Cast your cares on the Lord and He will sustain you; He will never let the righteous fall.

Matthew 5:4 Blessed are those who mourn, for they shall be comforted.

2 Corinthians 1:3-4 Blessed be the God and Father of our Lord Jesus Christ, the God of mercies and the God of all comfort, who comforts us in all our affliction, so that we may be able to comfort those who are in any affliction, with the comfort with which we ourselves are comforted by God.

Lamentations 3:31-33 For no one is cast off by the Lord forever. Though he brings grief, he will show compassion, so great is his unfailing love. For he does not willingly bring affliction or grief to anyone.

Things to think about

"Grief is the experience of coping with loss. Most of us think of grief as happening in the painful period following the death of a loved one. But grief can accompany any event that disrupts or challenges our sense of normalcy or ourselves. This includes the loss of connections that define us" (my.clevelandclinic.org/health/diseases/24787-grief). Grief can also be felt before a death of someone who is suffering from an illness, such as cancer or dementia. Several years ago, my mother died. She had suffered from a form of dementia that affected her behavior. She forgot how to behave in social situations, both in public and at home. My three sisters and I grieved the loss of her before her death because we lost the person that we knew and loved. Those who came to her funeral probably wondered why I had not broken down, but it was because I had already mourned the loss of her prior to her death. Each person mourns in their own unique way. There is no right or wrong way to mourn the loss of someone or something.

There are many biblical passages related to grief that are pertinent even in today's world.

Anger, Part 2

"Anger is a natural, instinctive response to threats. Some anger is necessary for our survival. Anger becomes a problem when you have trouble controlling it, causing you to say or do things you regret" (Santos-Longhurst, 2019). Anger is a very strong emotion that I have suffered from throughout life, and it may be a part of your life as well. As my family will tell you, I am unpredictable at times, especially when disagreements arise. Years ago I went to the doctor to get treatment for my anger issues, and I was put on an antidepressant. I learned recently that anger is as much a part of depression as depression is a part of anger (McLeod, LE, 2010, www.mcleodandmore.com).

"Anger is a feeling of displeasure that comes from various situations" (Pisegna, 191). Situations could include being cut off in traffic, being mad at the way someone else reacted, or even being angry at yourself for doing something dumb. Angry people "can become judgmental, overly critical of everything and everyone, cynical and pessimistic" (Pisegna, 192).

Why Anger Occurs

Anger can happen for a variety of reasons—someone pushes us too far, we get angry about a situation we are in, or we just don't feel that life is treating us fair. Stress, family problems and financial issues are frequent causes of anger (Santos-Longhurst, Feb. 4, 2019; www.healthline.com). Anger happens mostly because of a misunderstanding between two or more people, although you can also get angry at yourself for doing or saying something stupid, but it can also be a coping mechanism that you have learned early on (Meyer, J., 2012, 21-22). Mental health issues that can cause anger are depression, obsessive compulsive disorder, alcohol/drug abuse, ADHD, oppositional defiant disorder, bipolar disorder, intermittent explosive disorder, and grief (Santos-Longhurst, 2019). Another possible explanation for anger issues includes brain injury, such as traumatic brain injury, stroke, brain tumors, and other acquired brain injuries. Professional football players, boxers, and soccer players who have had multiple concussions have had emotional disturbances as well as other conditions (e.g., Depression and CTE). Traumatic brain injuries have been associated with an elevated incidence of Alzheimer disease and other dementias and a reduced age of onset for Alzheimer's (www.brainline.org/article/repetitive-head-injury).

According to Pisegna (194), anger happens when I

a) can't control things and people in my life
b) life doesn't meet my expectations

c) people irritate me and do things differently than I would do them

d) disappointments and injustice occur

e) don't get my way.

Even though he states that these are situations that cause him to get angry, I believe that most, if not all of these situations, cause anger in all of us.

Ways Anger is Expressed

There are many ways that anger is expressed. Of course, we think first about yelling and screaming, possibly throwing things or being verbally or physically abusive toward others (Santos-Longhurst, 2019), but giving someone the cold shoulder, avoiding people or situations, misusing Scripture and blaming others for how we feel (Meyer, J, 2012, pp. 45-53) are other ways that anger can be expressed. Other ways include negative self-talk, self-harm, and isolating yourself from others, or even being sarcastic or making snide remarks (Santos-Longhurst, 2019).

When anger is "mild and expressed in a constructive, nonhostile manner, anger may lead to positive outcomes such as expressing important feelings, identifying problems, redressing concerns, and motivating effective behavior. However, when intense and expressed in hostile, aggressive, or other dysfunctional ways, anger has been implicated in many problems"

(Deffenbecher, Oetting, and DiGuiseppe, 2002, 262), including partner violence/marital abuse, abusive parenting patterns, physical issues such as heart disease, school violence and bullying, among others (Deffenbecher, Oetting, and DiGuiseppe, 2002, 262). Mental health issues that can occur along with anger are anxiety, depression, and alcohol problems (Deffenbecher, Oetting, and DiGiuseppe, 263). Although only problems with alcohol are discussed in this article, it could also be assumed that drug abuse of either prescription or illegal drugs could also be issues.

Frustration

While anger and frustration are very similar, frustration is "often due to disappointment when an effort of observation does not work out as expected or anticipated" (Johnson, J., 2019; www.angermanagementexpert.co.uk/frustration-anger). Common reactions to frustration are "feeling overwhelmed or totally defeated" (Johnson, J., 2019). Frustration might be seen as anger turned inward (toward oneself), while anger could be seen as an outward emotion, an emotion that is expressed toward something or someone.

Similarities of the two emotions are that they are:

a) An emotional response and feeling and maybe be considered in a negative way
b) Can cause annoyance and evoke a physical reaction

c) When external stimuli are conflicting and not occurring as we anticipated we become frustrated or angry as a reaction.

d) We will probably need to exert some control or restraint in the way in which we respond. (Johnson, J., 2019)

The key difference between frustration and anger, however, is that "frustration can cause us to feel upset and vulnerable whereas anger may cause us to react in a more physical manner" (Johnson, J., 2019).

<u>Anger Management</u>

There are several effective ways to manage anger. Included are: a) recognizing your anger early, b) taking a timeout, c) deep breathing, d) exercise, e) once calm, expressing your anger in an assertive but nonconfrontational manner, f) thinking of the consequences, and g) visualization (www.therapistaid.com, 2012). Other methods, such as relaxation techniques or meditation, cognitive techniques (e.g., CBT), and social skills, are also helpful (Deffenbecher, Oetting, and DiGuiseppe, 2002, 268-272).

It is also suggested that counseling or psychotherapy can be effective for anger management, including cognitive-behavioral therapy and group therapy (Deffenbacher, Oetting, and DiGiuseppe, 263-264), although other forms of therapy are developed frequently. Beck Institute has developed a 7-step process for anger management, which includes:

a) Recognize the breaking of a should rule.

b) Examine what really hurts or scares us.

c) Respond to the hot, anger driven, reactive thoughts with cooler, more level-headed, reflective thoughts.

d) Respond to the anger arousal itself by practicing forms of relaxation, or to redefine the anger itself.

e) Examine the beliefs that turn anger into aggression.

f) Examine the specific dysfunctional behaviors that arise.

g) Reduce resentment and guilt.

(www.beckinstitute.org/seven-steps-anger)

"Breaking anger into steps that can enable us to recognize control, and give us more choices regarding both intervention and prevention" (www.beckinstitute.org/seven-steps-anger).

Biblical Study

"Refrain from anger and turn from wrath; do not fret—it leads only to evil" (Psalms 37:8; NIV).

"In your anger do not sin: Do not let the sun go down while you are still angry, and do not give the devil a foothold" (Ephesians 4:26-27; NIV).

"My dear brothers and sisters, take note of this: Everyone should be quick to listen, slow to speak, and slow to become angry, because human anger does not produce the righteousness that God desires. Therefore, get rid of all moral filth and the evil that is so prevalent and humbly accept the word planted in you, which can save you "(James 1:19-21; NIV).

All of these verses are telling us to control our anger, that through controlling the way we react we are able to allow God into our lives, rather than the devil.

The following two verses are for when you are frustrated and have lost faith. **"Trust in the Lord with all your heart and lean not on your own understanding; in all your ways submit to him, and he will make your paths straight" (Proverbs 3:5-6; NIV).** We all need to learn this, but especially when we are frustrated and don't know which way to turn. Learning to trust God is very important!

"Therefore, since we have been justified through faith, we have peace with God through our Lord Jesus Christ, through whom we have gained access by faith into this grace in which we now stand. And we boast in the hope of the glory of God. Not only so, but we also glory in our sufferings, because we know that suffering produces perseverance; perseverance, character; and character, hope. And hope does not put us to shame, because God's love has been poured out into our hearts through the Holy Spirit, who has been given to us" (Romans

5:1-5; NIV). By having faith in God, we are able to deal with our frustrations and anger more effectively. By persevering through the frustrations that we have, we are able to figure out why things are not working the way we want, and find new ways to do things.

Things to Think About

Anger is a very strong emotion, and it can be expressed in many ways, including against others and against ourselves. Dealing with anger in a constructive way takes a lot of work. Medication and/or counseling are some effective ways to deal with anger issues. Other ways include positive self-talk, journaling when you are angry, reading the Bible and praying, and discussing in a calm manner why you are angry. Easier said than done, I know, but if we work on constructive ways to express anger, and do it in a calm manner, dealing with anger will lead to our being healthier physically, mentally, and emotionally. What are other ways that you can deal with your anger appropriately?

Forgiveness

When we are angry or stressed, sometimes we yell at others, belittle others, or let our emotions get the better of us. It is at these times that forgiveness comes into the equation. How do we get to the point where we need to forgive ourselves or forgive others? It is one thing to accept an apology from someone who has hurt you, but forgiving yourself is completely different. Sometimes a difficult situation has caused us to feel a great deal of pain, and forgiveness is hard to give because of the situation. It is hard to let go of the hurt.

Forgiving ourselves is extremely difficult, especially if we have done something that goes completely against our own values. How do you forgive yourself after doing something horrible is difficult Megan Hale (www.mindbodygreen.com) has several suggestions:

a) "Become clear on your morals and values as they are right now.
b) Realize the past is the past.
c) Create a "re-do."
d) Realize you did the best you could at the time.
e) Start acting in accordance with your morals and values.
f) Identify your biggest regrets.

g) Tackle the big ones.

h) Turn the page.

i) Cut yourself some slack.

j) Move toward self-love." (Hale, www.mindbodygreen.com)

"You are more than your past mistakes, and I promise you, you are so worth it" (Hale, www.mindbodygreen.com)! Because we as humans are constantly changing our opinions on given issues, what may have been true last year for us may not still be true for us.

I have had problems forgiving myself for getting involved with the wrong person. Because of that person, I got arrested, spent four months in jail, and was sentenced to 5 years of probation. Will I ever get past it? I am trying to on a daily basis, but there are those who are not so quick to forgive so that I can move on with my life. I have accepted what I did, and I will not be getting in trouble again, but it still hurts that the arrest is haunting me even a year later because it is difficult for me to get employment. I am working part-time, but I am supposed to be working full-time. Getting others to look past the arrest is difficult.

Forgiving others can also be very difficult. In the last couple of years, I had finally figured out that holding someone else accountable for the anxiety that I have had over the years was not healthy or meaningful. I had been bullied by someone during my middle school years, and several years ago I had to take one of my children to a weekly catechism class. The classroom where I had experienced the bullying was the same classroom that I had to take my son to, and every time I took him to class, I had major anxiety about going there. I was the only one in my house that could drive at that time, so it was up to me to get my son to class. Last year, 35 years after the bullying occurred, I finally was able to forgive the person in my heart. I still have some anxiety issues, but I have them under control now. I am able to cope with them better because of forgiving the person and learning other coping skills that do not include blaming others.

Meyer (2012) gave several good examples about the way unforgiveness affects the relationships we have with others. First, an unforgiving person always keeps score. They know how many times a person has done something wrong. Next, the unforgiving person boasts of his good behavior. We all know people who brag about the good things they do. Comparing ourselves to others is another way of doing this. Third, the unforgiving person complains. The person is jealous of others and the good things that have happened to other people. Next, being unforgiving alienates you from others. How? Think about a person that you have something against. You have complained about the person to your spouse, but the spouse is having none of it. He or she attempts to tell you good things about the person, but instead of listening, you tune out your spouse, thereby alienating yourself from not just the person you complained about, but also your spouse. The next thing an unforgiving person does is talking about the wrong that was done to us. Finally, an unforgiving person resents the blessings enjoyed by the other person. If you think about it, all of these things were done by the older brother in the parable of the Prodigal Son (Luke 15:11-32).

Biblical Study

The Bible gives us many passages about forgiveness, and how God's forgiveness is different than human forgiveness. Many times someone will hold on to the hurt and anger because they do not feel that they can forgive. However, by letting go of the anger and forgiving we are able to help ourselves on our own journey. Forgiving others will bring forgiveness to you!

"Therefore I tell you, whatever you ask for in prayer, believe that you have received it, and it will be yours. And when you stand praying, if you hold anything against anyone, forgive them, so that your Father in heaven may forgive your sins" (Mark 11:24-26; NIV).

"Therefore, as God's chosen people, holy and dearly loved, clothe yourselves with compassion, kindness, humility, gentleness, and patience. Bear with each other and forgive one another if any of you has a grievance against someone. Forgive as the Lord forgave you. And over all these virtues put on love, which binds them all together in perfect unity" (Colossians 3:12-14; NIV). So we are to be good and kind, gentle, patient, humble, and forgiving. I know it is difficult to be this way given the stressors that are in your life, but it can be done.

In Joyce Meyer's book, <u>Do Yourself a Favor...Forgive</u>, she talks about Eva Kor, who suffered unthinkable things at Auschwitz. Ms. Kor forgave those who killed her family, among millions of others. Ms. Kor stated: "Forgiveness is nothing more and nothing less than an act of self-healing—an act of self-empowerment. And I immediately felt a burden of pain was lifted from my shoulder—that I was no longer a victim of Auschwitz, that I was no longer a prisoner of my tragic past, that I was finally free.... I call forgiveness the modern miracle medicine. You don't have to belong to an HMO. There is no co-pay; therefore, everybody can afford it. There are no side effects. And if you don't like the way you feel without the pain of the past, you can always go and take your pain back" (Meyer, 100-101). If she can forgive such an atrocity toward her own family, I believe that we can forgive those who have hurt us.

"Let the wicked forsake their ways and the unrighteous their thoughts. Let them turn to the Lord, and he will have mercy on them, and to our God, for he will freely pardon" (Isaiah 55:7; NIV). Turning toward God is the only way that we will be forgiven, and he will forgive us for all our sins.

"This then is how you should pray: "'Our Father in heaven, hallowed be your name, your kingdom come, your will be done, on earth as it is in heaven. Give us today our daily bread. And forgive us our debts, as we also have forgiven our debtors. And lead us not into temptation, but deliver us from the evil one'" (Matthew 6:9-13; NIV). Forgive others like the Father forgives us.

The modern day Our Father:

Our Father, who art in heaven, hallowed be thy name. Thy kingdom come, thy will be done, on earth as it is in heaven. Give us this day our daily bread, and forgive us our trespasses as we forgive those who trespass against us. And lead us not into temptation, but deliver us from evil. Amen.

Things to Think About

We get hurt by others, offended, so easily. Is it worth the internal hurt to hold on to the grievances against us? Forgiving those who have offended us is not easy, but it can be done. Who and what do you need to forgive? Who has hurt you? Have you done anything that you need to forgive yourself for?

Last year I was thinking about a lot of things that had happened to me growing up and even as an adult. It took me 35 years to forgive one particular person who had hurt me emotionally. Although I do not plan on being friends with her, I have forgiven her in my heart. Through forgiving her I have become more accepting of those that have hurt myself and others.

Depression

Depression is a very real and widely misunderstood mental illness because it can manifest in many ways, from backtalk and anger, physical aggression, hopelessness, and of course, sadness. According to the DSM-5 (2013), there are several types of depressive disorders, but for simplicity we will focus on Major Depressive Disorder. The depressed person has a depressed mood most of the day, nearly every day, has little to no interest or pleasure in all, or almost all, activities, significant weight loss when not dieting or weight gain, insomnia or hypersomnia nearly every day, psychomotor agitation or retardation nearly every day, fatigue or loss of energy nearly every day, feelings of worthlessness or excessive or inappropriate guilt, diminished ability to think or concentrate, or indecisiveness, nearly every day, and recurrent thoughts of death (APA,160-161). The symptoms cause "significant distress or impairment in social, occupational, or other areas of functioning," (APA, 161). The episode is not attributable to the physiological effects of a substance or to another medical condition. The episode is not better explained by another form of mental illness. Finally, there has never been a manic or hypomanic episode (APA, 161).

Treatment of Depression

Countless people suffer from depression, myself included. What can be done about depression? Many things! But we have to first want to get out of the depression and approach it in an objective manner.

Treatment of depression frequently involves either counseling, medication, or a combination of the two, although there are some that try a more holistic approach, such as supplements, that help with the natural balance of chemicals in the brain. There are several ways to treat depression holistically. A holistic approach would include considering why you are depressed, and if you can do anything about why. Are you having trouble at work or at home? What situations make you stressed? Another way to treat depression holistically is to exercise.

Eating foods that enhance the serotonin in the brain helps as well, foods like salmon, sardines, healthy fats such as coconut oil, eating a high protein diet, avoid caffeine, getting some sunshine, and taking mood-enhancing supplements such as 5-HTP, St. John's Wort, and fish oil, among others, may help.

Meditation or guided imagery may help you as well, since these tend to help a person to relax and focus. Get a physical and find out if your hormones are in balance. If your thyroid, adrenal gland, or sex hormones are not in balance, this can affect your mood.

Being authentic/real with others is important too! If you "wear a mask" around others (pretending to be something that you are not), you are not being real or true to yourself.

Finally, talking with a counselor, psychologist, or life coach can be a big help. If you still need antidepressants after trying these holistic options, take them. Don't beat yourself up about having to take medication (Rankin, L., 11 Natural Treatments, www.psychologytoday.com). Depression is as much a physical illness as high blood pressure!

Recovery from depression, or any mental illness, is a multistep process, no matter what the treatment. According to www.beyondblue.org, there are 5 steps:

a) Shock
b) Denial
c) Despair and Anger
d) Acceptance
e) Coping.

Shock is the feeling you get when you first get diagnosed. You are in a feeling of disbelief, thinking things such as "How can this be? Did I do something wrong?". You then deny that it is possible the diagnosis is correct. You are sad and angry for what you feel is a fault of you, or you may feel that someone else is to blame for your illness. You might even do research about the diagnosis at this stage, find out why you have this particular diagnosis. Then you accept that the diagnosis is true after you have thought about it. Finally, you cope with the diagnosis and the difficulties that come along with it. This acceptance of whatever the diagnosis or difficulty is brings about the beginning of self-acceptance. By accepting the difficulty you are becoming more in tune with your true persona. You become happier through this acceptance. This self-acceptance, however, does not take away the diagnosis of depression, but allows you to be able to cope better with the diagnosis.

Biblical Study

"He heals the brokenhearted and binds up their wounds" (Psalms 147:3; NIV).

"Even youths grow tired and weary, and young men stumble and fall; but those who hope in the Lord will renew their strength. They will soar on wings like eagles; they will run and not grow weary, they will walk and not be faint" (Isaiah 40:30-31; NIV).

"So do not fear, for I am with you; do not be dismayed, for I am your God. I will strengthen you and help you; I will uphold you with my righteous right hand" (Isaiah 41:10; NIV).

"Create in me a pure heart, O God, and renew a steadfast spirit within me. Do not cast me from your presence or take your Holy Spirit from me. Restore to me the joy of your salvation and grant me a willing spirit to sustain me" (Psalms 51:10-12; NIV).

"My sacrifice, O God, is a broken spirit; a broken and contrite heart you, God, will not despise (Psalms 51:17; NIV).

Each of these passages confronts the topic of depression in different ways. While the passage from Psalms talks about God helping those who are down, the passages from Isaiah talks about how believing in God can bring you strength to get through the depression when it hits you. Prayer, such as in Psalms 51:10-12 and verse 17, allow you to give control of the situation to God, who will work within us to get us through the darkest parts of our lives.

Things to Think About

Depression is very real. It can become quite overwhelming, and anger as well as suicidal thoughts may come about as a result. Do not be afraid to ask for the help you need to get through the depression.

I post positive sayings and pictures all around me so that I remind myself to stay positive and focused. One of the sayings is: "I am Me! I am Somebody! I Love Me! I Can Get Past the Sadness!" It is important to stay focused when working to overcome depression. Notice I say working, not trying. If you are only trying, you tend to give up easily. If you are working toward getting better, that means it is a goal worth achieving, a goal worth working toward. So don't try, but rather do! There is a saying from Nike™, the shoe and apparel brand—Just Do It! That is exactly what you should do! Get working on a goal and do what you need to do to get past it!

Consider the reasons for the depression, as well as what you can do about it. What can you do to get yourself through the situation? What are some goals (a purpose) you can work toward so you are able to focus on something more positive?

"Our thoughts feed our feelings, so if you feel discontent, the way to get over it is to change your thinking. Think about what you do have instead of what you don't have" (Meyer, 43). Essentially, change your mindset. Work at becoming more positive. Find your purpose and work toward your goals! That way you can gain happiness!

Anxiety

Anxiety is another mental illness that occurs frequently in those who feel unaccepted by others. Why? Because they work themselves up thinking about why they are not accepted by certain people. Anxiety often occurs in the depressed person. It is because both the depressed person and the anxious person overthink about a situation.

Like depression, there are several disorders that are anxiety-related. However, the ones I will focus on are Generalized Anxiety Disorder and Panic Disorder. Generalized Anxiety Disorder (GAD) has several qualifiers:

a) Excessive anxiety and worry (apprehensive expectation), occurring more days than not for at least 6 months, about a number of events or activities.

b) The individual finds it difficult to control the worry.

c) The anxiety and worry are associated with three (or more) of the following six symptoms:

   a. Restlessness or feeling keyed up or on edge

   b. Being easily fatigued.

   c. Difficulty concentrating or mind going blank.

   d. Irritability.

   e. Muscle tension.

f. Sleep disturbance.

g. The anxiety, worry, or physical symptoms cause clinically significant distress or impairment in social, occupational, or other important areas of functioning.

h. The disturbance is not attributable to the physiological effects of a substance or another medical condition.

i. The disturbance is not better explained by another mental disorder (APA, DSM-5, 222).

Social anxiety occurs often when one suffers rejection because it causes an immense pain or fear that "is so powerful that it explains why some people would rather avoid social interaction than experience the threat of rejection or social failure" (Schwartz, www.MentalHelp.net). Schwartz suggests that those who suffer from social anxiety, shyness, or other forms of anxiety to seek therapy, especially Cognitive Behavioral Therapy (CBT) and group therapy.

"In panic disorder, the individual experiences recurrent unexpected panic attacks and is persistently concerned or worried about having more panic attacks or changes his or her behavior in maladaptive ways because of the panic attacks. Panic attacks are abrupt surges of intense fear or intense discomfort that reach a peak within minutes, accompanied by physical and/or cognitive symptoms (DSM-5, 190). Physical and cognitive symptoms that can occur during a panic attack are:

a) Palpitations, pounding heart, or accelerated heart rate

b) Sweating

c) Trembling or shaking

d) Sensations of shortness of breath or smothering

e) Feelings of choking

f) Chest pain or discomfort

g) Nausea or abdominal distress

h) Feeling dizzy, unsteady, light-headed, or faint

i) Chills or heat sensations

j) Paresthesias (numbness or tingling sensations)

k) Derealization (feelings of unreality) or depersonalization
   (being detached from oneself)

l) Fear of losing control or "going crazy"

m) Fear of dying (DSM-5, 208).

At least 4 of these symptoms must occur, and cannot be better explained by another mental disorder, medical condition, medication, or substance (DSM-5, 209).

Worry

While worrying happens to everyone at one time or another, if there is excessive worry, anxiety and panic can become an issue (McKay, Davis, and Fanning, 69 and 85). "Fear is the emotional response to real of perceived imminent threat, whereas anxiety is anticipation of future threat" (DSM-V, 189). "You have a serious problem with worry if you regularly experience any of the following:

a) Chronic anxiety about future dangers or threats
b) Consistently making negative predictions about the future
c) Often overestimating the probability or seriousness of bad things happening
d) Inability to stop repeating the same worries over and over
e) Escaping worry by distracting yourself or avoiding certain situations

Having difficulty using worry constructively to produce solutions to problems" (McKay, Davis, and Fanning, 69).

Panic

Panic involves "an overwhelming feeling of terror that you could die or completely lose control" (McKay, Davis, and Fanning, 85). Panic attacks "feature prominently within the anxiety disorders as a particular type of fear response" (DSM-V, 189), although panic attacks are seen across the psychological spectrum.

Coping with Anxiety

Handly and Neff (1985) suggest five principles in order to conquer fear, which in turn help with reducing and/or eliminating anxiety and panic:

a) Use the creative powers of your unconscious mind to help you change yourself.

b) Use visualizations and affirmations to change your self-image so that you feel confidence rather than fear.

c) Use rational and positive thinking to see yourself and events as they really are and also to visualize how you want them to be.

d) Act as if you are already the way you want to be.

e) Set goals to become the person you want to be (42).

While these are good guidelines to help deal with anxiety, I believe that prayer should be added as well. Why prayer? When we feel like there is a loss of control in whatever situation we are in, we feel stress. Anxiety skyrockets. One of the things my mother would tell me (frequently, I might add) is that when I was feeling worried or anxious about something, that I should pray about it. By praying and talking to God (or whoever you believe in), you are letting him have control, allowing Him to lead the way.

Biblical Study

"Not that I have already obtained all this, or have already arrived at my goal, but I press on to take hold of that for which Christ Jesus took hold of me. Brothers and sisters, I do not consider myself yet to have taken hold of it. But one thing I do: Forgetting what is behind and straining toward what is ahead, I press on toward the goal to win the prize for which God has called me heavenward in Christ Jesus (Philippians 3:12-14; NIV). Worrying about the past will get you nowhere, but working toward your goals is what needs doing. However, do not allow stress and anxiety about the future to take hold of you!

"Rejoice in the Lord always. I shall say it again: rejoice! Your kindness shall be known to all. The Lord is near. Have no anxiety at all, but in everything, by prayer and petition, with thanksgiving, make your requests known to God. Then the peace of God that surpasses all understanding will guard your hearts and minds in Christ Jesus" (Philippians 4:4-7; NABRE). Prayers of thanksgiving when we are anxious or stressed gives us a good basis for getting us back into a more positive outlook. By stating what we are thankful for, we are changing our mindset.

Prayer for Anxiety and Stress:

Oh Lord, Let me hear you. My soul is weary. Worry, fear and doubt surround me on every side. Yet your sweet mercy cannot be held back from those that cry out to you. Hear my cry! Let me trust in your mercy. Show me how. Free me. Free me from anxiety and stress, that I may find rest in your loving arms! Amen. (www.prayerforanxiety.com)

Things to Think About

Worry, anxiety, and panicking do you no good. Much like depression, which is living in the past to excess, worry, anxiety, and panic are living in the future to an excessive amount. In order to get past the excess worry and anxiety (in addition to panic), one must find a productive way to cope with worry and anxiousness. Ways to cope that I have found helpful are journaling or writing of any sort, talking it out with a friend, listening to soothing music (I prefer classical), and meditation. What do you do that helps you cope with worry, anxiety, and panic?

Suicide

Suicide is seen as an extreme reaction to rejection. Those that feel alone and rejected are often very depressed about the situation and become suicidal. Because of the fact that they are also very good at hiding what they are truly feeling, those that are depressed are often not recognized as depressed or suicidal. In a Norwegian study (Nauert, 2018), rejection and a sense of failure were looked at as possibly leading to suicide when ten young men had taken their lives. These young men were "apparently well-functioning young men" (Nauert, 2018), and they had no prior sign of mental illness. Shame and rejection appeared to be factors in these suicides.

Those that are suicidal frequently cannot get past the negative thoughts that are going through their head and obsess over the failures they have had (even those that are minor failures) rather than looking at the positive things that have happened, their successes in life. In addition, those that are suicidal don't want to die, but rather just have the pain (whether mental or physical) to go away.

Alex Lickerman (2010) discussed the six reasons why people attempt suicide. He found that they are either a) depressed, b) psychotic, c) impulsive, d) crying out for help, e) have a philosophical desire to die, or e) have made a mistake. Although I find that these are probably true, it really does not cover the whole picture on the suicidality of the individual. Suicide is a very personal decision, and as such we should try to fully understand the person before they attempt, not after they succeed killing themselves. Too often we understand after the fact when we should have been attempting to understand the person and trying to prevent their deciding to end it all. The main reason so many attempt/commit suicide is the lack of control they have in their own lives. Their death is the one thing that they can have complete control over through their choice of choosing suicide, and the method they choose to take to end it all.

Control of something in their life when they feel that they have none is often a reason for suicidal thoughts. We have control over our actions and the way we respond (Glasser, 1984, 45), unless we are being forced into doing something. We are "always trying to choose to behave in a way that gives us the most effective control over our lives" (Glasser, 1998, 71). So, not only do we attempt to control ourselves, but we also try to control others to our own benefit! There are many ways to regain control within our lives, but I found the following to be helpful—the acronym STOP. How does it work?

a) Slow your breathing and enter into a quick and simple mindfulness practice.

141

b) Take note, by noticing what you are experiencing in the present moment.

c) Open up, and allow yourself to feel without judgment or avoidance.

d) Pursue your values, by deciding what the best course of action is based on your most important values (www.positivepsychologyprogram.com/act-acceptance-and-commitment-therapy).

By utilizing this method we are recognizing each of the core processes that were mentioned previously regarding ACT. We regain control of whatever situation we are in, and we are able to bring about a more positive mindset and hopefully decreasing the depression and anxiety that is usually a cause for suicidal thoughts.

There are four components that make up our "total behavior," and these components are essential to the control we have within our lives (Glasser, 1984, 46-47). Doing, Thinking, Feeling, and Physiology are the four components, and I will explain now how each of these is essential.

Doing, as Glasser (1984, 46-47) explains, is an action, a behavior in which we deliberately control our body in order to do what we want it to do. Exercise can be seen as a positive or negative activity, while lying in bed can be seen as either a positive or negative activity as well, depending on the reason behind each action. In the depressed person, lying in bed can be seen as negative because the action itself allows us to dwell on negative thoughts and feelings. Dreams can also be what we visualize ourselves doing in the immediate or foreseeable future. In the positive person, lying in bed might be a good time to reflect on the good things that have happened during that day.

Thinking involves voluntarily generating thoughts or involuntarily generating thoughts through dreaming (Glasser, 1984, 46). You can mull over something like a math problem, or think about what you are going to do when you get home after you are done working. Or you can dream (usually while asleep). These dreams are usually bits and pieces of things that are important to you, or fears that you have, or thoughts that happen as your mind consolidates the information in your brain about things that happened that day. Unfortunately these thoughts and dreams are not always positive, and those negative thoughts can become stuck in our heads. Thoughts can bring about anxiety and depression, or happiness.

Feelings are emotional thoughts, and these thoughts can be positive or negative. I can feel anxious around certain people while happy around others. The anxiety can show up as tenseness in the shoulders, stomach upset, or even as leg cramps or muscle spasms. These feelings—the happiness, grief, anxiety, sadness, or excitement, among others—affect how we respond to others

(Glasser, 1984, 47). Depression, many of us understand, is more than sadness. Yes, we may cry when we are depressed, but many times we may also just be quiet and shut down. At those times we mull over our thoughts, wonder how it would feel to do certain things, like harming ourselves, or killing ourselves. What I tell others when they start talking about suicide, for example, is that they have a greater purpose through the difficulties they have encountered, that killing themselves will just bring more pain to those who survive. Although more research needs to be done regarding ACT as a form of therapy with those who are suicidal, it shows a great deal of promise in the way it works with other mental health issues.

Physiology is how our body responds both voluntarily and involuntarily to the emotions that are felt (Glasser, 1984, 47). Are you sweating or clenching your fists? Is your stomach in knots? In some people, like myself, the tenseness is felt throughout my upper back and in my stomach. As a result my digestive system works overtime and causes myself to need to use the bathroom frequently.

In 2014 there was a pilot study done to see how ACT helped those who were suicidal. Although a small population was used (only 35 participants), ACT seemed to decrease the occurrence of suicidal thoughts (Ducasse, Rene, Beziat, et al, 2014). Although more research needs to be done regarding using ACT as a form of therapy, the results show positive results with its use, and if it is effective in the long-term. Suicidal thoughts tend to decrease when you are focused on something else, like a project, because you are thinking about what you need to do to complete the project. However, if you become overwhelmed by the project—if it is a work project, for example—you may become more suicidal.

Biblical Study

Suicidal thoughts often come because depression or anxiety has become overwhelming. Even though some religions have taught that suicide is bad, or against the church's teaching, many times suicide is just a means to escape the reality that the person lives in. Although there are some that truly want to die, I find that this is likely to be few as opposed to those who just want to escape the world in which they are living.

"I remember my affliction and my wandering, the bitterness and the gall. I will remember them, and my soul is downcast within me Yet this I call to mind and therefore I have hope: Because of the Lord's great love we are not consumed, for his compassions never fail. They are new every morning; great is your faithfulness. I say to myself, 'The Lord is my portion; therefore I will wait for him'" (Lamentations 3:19-24).

"I will exalt you, O Lord, for you lifted me out of the depths and did not let my enemies gloat over me. O Lord my God, I called to you for help and you healed me. O Lord, you brought

me up from the grave; you spared me from going down into the pit. Sing to the Lord, you saints of his; praise his holy name. For his anger lasts only a moment, but his favor lasts a lifetime; weeping may remain for a night, but rejoicing comes in the morning. When I felt secure, I said, 'I will never be shaken.' O Lord, when you favored me, you made my mountain stand firm; but when you hid your face, I was dismayed. To you , O Lord, I called; to the Lord I cried for mercy; 'What gain is there in my destruction, in my going down into the pit? Will the dust praise you? Will it proclaim your faithfulness? Hear, O Lord, and be merciful to me; O Lord, be my help.' You turned my wailing into dancing; you removed my sackcloth and clothed me with joy, that my heart may sing to you and not be silent. O Lord my God, I will give you thanks forever" (Psalms 30; NIV). Reading this particular Psalm gives me hope, that I will not always be in the pit of despair. Praying to God, letting him know your worries and concerns, allows him to begin working on getting you through the trouble. Suicidal thoughts are the pit, and God will help you get out if you let him.

"Be merciful to me, O Lord, for I am in distress; my eyes grow weak with sorrow, my soul and my body with grief. My life is consumed by anguish and my years by groaning; my strength fails because of my affliction, and my bones grow weak. Because of all my enemies, I am the utter contempt of my neighbors; I am a dread to my friends—those who see me on the street flee from me. I am forgotten by them as though I were dead; I have become like broken pottery. For I hear the slander of many; there is terror on every side; they conspire against me and plot to take my life. But I trust in you, O Lord; I say, 'You are my God.' My times are in your hands; deliver me from my enemies and from those who pursue me. Let your face shine on your servant; save me in your unfailing love. Let me not be put to shame, O Lord, for I have cried out to you; but let the wicked be put to shame and lie silent in the grave" (Psalms 31:9-17; NIV).

Things to Think About

Control, like I said before, is something that many of those with depression or anxiety feel that is necessary in their lives. If they lack control of an area in their life such as work or a relationship with someone, the negative feelings tend to increase, bringing about even more intense negative thinking. This is where the suicidal thoughts enter the picture if the person has not learned some good coping skills. The uncontrolled thoughts and feelings take over, telling the person that they are not good enough, that nothing they do will be right, and they believe that they are a horrible person. The person who has some good friends will be less likely to let the negative thoughts to interfere because they have people that they can depend on to help them through the situation. Those that have no good friends or little social life will dwell on this fact and believe that no one needs them, that they have no purpose. This is not only false, but it is also difficult to get out of one's head. Once the negativity begins, it is hard to stop it.

Hope

You may ask, "Why is there a chapter on hope, and why is it placed after the chapter on suicide?" The reason is this: Although we as humans suffer from each of the previously mentioned difficulties, including suicidal thoughts, once we get past them we have hope within us. Hope gives us a reason to believe that we can get through the difficult times, and the will to survive! In this chapter on hope, I hope to give you ways to find the inner strength to get past the rejection, the stress, the depression, the anxiety, and the suicidal thoughts.

Archbishop Jose H. Gomez spoke about hope in the book Beautiful Hope, stating that "Hope is the theological virtue that enables us to keep our eyes on heaven—even during those times when our sufferings and trials make our lives here on earth seem like a living hell" (Kelly, 2017, 97). Hope, then, allows us to look past our trials in life and look forward to death because we know what is past life.

Another definition of hope is to believe, desire, or trust. Depression or despair, on the other hand, is sadness, gloom, or dejection. Being depressed, in other words, is a lack of hope. It is when we have hope that good things are more likely to happen, although bad things can happen when we are hopeful as well. It is all in how we perceive the situation we are in. Do you feel that things will get better for you? Or do you feel that nothing will ever be good? Perception is everything! You do not have to be the eternal optimist, but know that you will get through each challenge as it comes your way.

What does hope have to do with acceptance? "Acceptance is looking toward the future and the possibilities that it holds" (www.hopeforthebrokenhearted.com/acceptance). This means that looking forward to the future is a sign of hope. Hope means many things to many people. We hope to get a new job, or get accepted into a university, or maybe even hope that our children become successful. Hope is also staying positive during difficult times, and accepting the consequences of a decision, even if it is one we do not want.

Faith is also very important. Our faith is tested frequently, and I have to say that my faith has been tested quite a bit recently. However, after living in jail for four months, and reading the Bible daily while in there, my faith increased substantially. I even promised God that I would begin going back to church when I got out of jail. I followed through, and I have been attending mass every Sunday for over a year now. There have been times that the priest's sermon was so touching that it made me cry! I truly felt that God was speaking to me.

Biblical Study

Hope and faith, I believe, are two sides of the same coin. Without hope, we have no faith. Without faith we have no hope. They are two sides, but neither can exist without the other. When we go through a difficult time (chaos), we must have faith and hope in order to get to the other side (Pisegna, 108). The biblical definition of faith comes from the book of Hebrews: "Now faith is confidence in what we hope for and assurance about what we do not see" (Hebrews 11:1; NIV). Faith is discussed many times throughout the Bible, but one place that tells us more about it: "The Lord is my light and my salvation—whom shall I fear? The Lord is the stronghold of my life—of whom shall I be afraid" (Psalm 27:1-2; NIV)? Another place is in Philippians: "Do not be anxious about anything, but in every situation, by prayer and petition, with thanksgiving, present your requests to God. And the peace of God, which transcends all understanding, will guard your hearts and your minds in Christ Jesus" (Philippians 4:6-7; NIV). This is what we mean by faith, that God will listen to your prayers and answer them. He will keep you calm and able to face each challenge.

Hope is discussed many times within the Bible. One verse about hopefulness is "What then shall we say to this? If God is for us, who can be against us? He who did not spare his own Son but handed him over for us all, how will he not also give us everything else along with him" (Romans 8:31-32; NABRE)? Hope is different than faith. How? Let's look at a couple of different passages: "We are hard pressed on every side, but not crushed; perplexed, but not in despair; persecuted but not abandoned; struck down, but not destroyed" (2 Corinthians 4:8-9; NIV). This passage talks about how hope is vital even in difficult times. One may be frustrated but can still be hopeful. Another passage includes: "Therefore, since we have been justified through faith, we have peace with God through our Lord Jesus Christ, through whom we have gained access by faith into this grace in which we now stand. And we boast in the hope of the glory of God. Not only so, but we also glory in our sufferings, because we know that suffering produces perseverance; perseverance, character; and character, hope. And hope does not put us to shame, because God's love has been poured out into our hearts through the Holy Spirit, who has been given to us" (Romans 5:1-5; NIV).

Here is a passage that discusses both hope and faith (trust): "Accept whatever happens to you; in periods of humiliation be patient. For in fire gold is tested, and the chosen, in the crucible of humiliation. Trust in God and he will help you; make your ways straight and hope in him. You that fear the Lord, wait for his mercy, do not stray lest you fall. You that fear the Lord, trust in him and your reward will not be lost. You that fear the Lord, hope for good things, for lasting joy and mercy." (Ben Sira 2:4-9 (Also known as Sirach); not in all Bibles; NABRE). This says a lot about

152

faith and acceptance. By trusting God we are putting our faith in God.

"Cast your care upon the Lord, who will give you support. He will never allow the righteous to stumble" (Psalms 55:32; NABRE).

"Do not fear: I am with you; do not be anxious: I am your God. I will strengthen you, I will help you, I will uphold you with my victorious right hand" (Isaiah 41:10; NABRE).

"May the God of hope fill you with all joy and peace as you trust in him, so that you may overflow with hope by the power of the Holy Spirit" (Romans 15:13; NIV). Hope, joy, and peace come from your trust in God, knowing that he will carry you through each challenge that you face.

"Therefore, my dear friends, as you have always obeyed—not only in my presence, but now much more in my absence—continue to work out your salvation with fear and trembling for it is God who works in you to will and to act in order to fulfill his good purpose" (Philippians 2:12-13; NIV).

"We who are strong ought to bear with the failings of the weak and not to please ourselves. Each of us should please our neighbors for their good, to build them up. For even Christ did not please himself but, as it is written: "The insults of those who insult you have fallen on me." For everything that was written in the past was written to teach us, so that through the endurance taught in the Scriptures and the encouragement they provide we might have hope. May the God who gives endurance and encouragement give you the same attitude of mind toward each other that Christ Jesus had, so that with one mind and one voice you may glorify the God and Father of our Lord Jesus Christ" (Romans 15:1-5; NIV).

"May the God of hope fill you with all joy and peace as you trust in him, so that you may overflow with hope by the power of the Holy Spirit (Romans 15:13; NIV)."

All of these verses give us hope. They let us know that God is with us, that we are never alone, and that he will help us get through each struggle. That is what hope is all about!

Things to Think About

Hope is essential to life. As a young girl, I was always trying to help others. I did not like it when I saw someone down or depressed. I would go up to the person (my 5-year-old self) and tell the person that things would get better, that life would turn around. I would try to give the person a sense of hope even then! Now, of course, I have lived many years, and even though I have my times of depression, I still attempt to offer hope to others. I hope that you have gotten something good out of this book! I believe that good things are always possible, and that by encouraging others to be who they are meant to be, we are offering hope.

Peace Within You

Living a peaceful life is something that we all strive for. Many times, however, living peacefully is lacking because it seems there are constant fights, arguments, and turmoil. Living peacefully does not mean that there is no arguing or fighting. Rather, it is living with empathy and understanding. By taking the time to understand another person and their point of view, we are becoming more peaceful. To have empathy means that you have the ability to understand and share the feelings of another; the capacity to understand or feel what another person is experiencing from within their frame of reference.

Why is empathy so important? For one thing, it allows you to feel an emotional connection to someone else. How we feel is very subjective. If I am feeling angry about something, the empathic person can look at the situation bit by bit, asking questions when needed, and figuring out exactly why I am angry. They can then, through understanding the difficulty, help me to understand better about what is going on in my head. Through analyzing the situation, the empathic person makes the troubled person feel important, rather than unwanted or unloved. It feels good when someone else can help us through the problem. Of course there will be times when you feel frustrated and misunderstood, but hopefully those are few and far between.

Inner peace is slightly different. Rather than another person empathizing with you, you are in a state of being mentally and spiritually at peace, with enough knowledge and understanding to keep yourself strong in the face of difficulty. It is a feeling of calmness rather than chaos. You are fine with who you are as a person, and you are not struggling by becoming someone you are not. So being at peace with yourself means that you understand who you are! Essentially, inner peace is empathy turned inward.

Prior to becoming an archbishop, Fulton J. Sheen (1955) wrote a book called Way to Inner Peace. In this book he wrote about humility as being necessary to have inner peace. This work, even though it is over 60 years old, gives many insights that are relevant even today. First off, "The humble man knows himself as he really is, for he judges himself as he really is, for he judges himself as he judges time, by a standard outside himself, namely, God and His Moral Law" (12). Humility, which apparently was not popular even back in the 1950s, is still uncommon today, "because men have forgotten the Greatness of God. By expanding our puny little self to the infinite, we have made the true Infinity of God seem trivial. The less knowledge we have of anything the more insignificant it seems" (11). He goes on to say, "The psychological reason for the modern fondness for news which deflates others or brings out the evil in their lives is to solace uneasy consciences which are already laden with guilt. By finding others who apparently are more evil, one falsely believes he becomes better" (12).

By being humble and not believing oneself to be better than anyone else, we allow ourselves to experience the greatness of God in his infinite wisdom and being. If we consider the wreck that the world is in today, we see that by putting others before ourselves will get us into the habit of service to others, which will in turn help us to become humble and at peace within ourselves. This will bring about contentment, which will help us to control the desires that we have. We will be able to differentiate between wants and needs better (Sheen, 25-26).

Another Perspective

One of the prayers/hymns that I learned growing up is the Prayer of St. Francis of Assisi (also known as the Peace Prayer). Until recently I had never really analyzed the meaning of the prayer, but I believe that it is instruction on how to empathize with others and how to find inner peace. The prayer goes like this:

Lord, Make me an instrument of thy peace;

Where there is hatred, let me sow love;

Where there is injury, pardon;

Where there is doubt, faith;

Where there is despair, hope;

Where there is darkness, light;

And where there is sadness, joy.

O Divine Master, grant that I may not so much seek to be consoled as to console;

To be understood as to understand;

To be loved, as to love;

For it is in giving that we receive,

It is in pardoning that we are pardoned,

And it is in dying that we are born to eternal life.

What exactly does this prayer mean? As you can tell, everything is a paradox—hatred/love, injury (insult)/pardon (forgiveness), doubt/faith, despair/hope, darkness/light, and sadness/joy. He is asking God for his guidance when he finds or experiences times of distress so he can get to the other side of the difficulty. He wants to be more understanding of those that he serves, because it is obviously better to be understanding and caring rather than callous and destructive.

Biblical Study

There are several biblical passages that talk about peace, and not just the type of worldly peace, but rather the way to inner peace. In Isaiah there are two passages that I feel are crucial to feeling peace within us. Isaiah 26:3 (NIV) states: "You will keep in perfect peace those whose minds are steadfast, because they trust in you." So mental calmness is necessary to have so that others will trust you. Isaiah 42:16 (NIV) reads: "I will lead the blind by ways they have not known, along unfamiliar paths I will guide them; I will turn the darkness into light before them and make the rough places smooth. These are the things I will do; I will not forsake them." Those whose minds are going in a hundred different directions will have peace because God will lead the way when they are uncertain about which way to go.

In the New Testament there are several passages that related to peace as well. For example, in the book of John 8:12 (NIV) "When Jesus spoke again to the people, he said, 'I am the light of the world. Whoever follows me will never walk again in darkness, but will have the light of life.'" In John 14;27, it states "Peace I leave with you; my peace I give you. I do not give to you as the world gives. Do not let your hearts be troubled and do not be afraid. By following Jesus and believing in God, peace will come into our lives. The darkness and uncertainty will go away. In 2 Thessalonians 3:16, Paul writes, "Now may the Lord of peace himself give you peace at all times and in every way. The Lord be with all of you." So not only does Jesus wish us peace, but apostles such as Paul wish us peace as well.

Finally, in the book of James 1:5-8, is another passage that speaks about peace. "If any of you lacks wisdom, you should ask God, who gives generously to all without finding fault, and it will be given to you. But when you ask, you must believe and not doubt, because the one who doubts is like a wave of the sea, blown and tossed by the wind. That person should not expect to receive anything from the Lord. Such a person is double-minded and unstable in all they do." Not only should we believe and not doubt, but we should be stable and secure in our ways.

Things to Think About

How can we become a more empathic person? Listen, ask questions, and watch their body language. Stay calm and do not judge the person, just listen and become aware of how they are truly feeling. It is not a time to judge, but rather a time to help the person heal.

How can we become more at peace? Listen to yourself. Think about what you want, what you need. There are several ways to do this:

a) Writing down your thoughts (journaling) is a good way to start. Set it aside for a day or two and reread what you wrote. By rereading what your thoughts were, you will gain a better understanding of where you were mentally, and where you are now. Things change from minute to minute and day to day.

b) Talk with an understanding friend. Because they are a good friend, they will likely be able to listen without judging, and maybe even offer some insight later. Also, you may consider talking to a priest, minister, or rabbi, as they may be able to offer some other insights as well.

c) Reading the Bible can help as well. By reading and thinking about what the person is saying that relates to your life, you will be better able to focus on the things that truly matter in your life.

d) Forgiving the person, even in your mind, is also a great way to bring peace to you. Dwelling on the hurt that someone did to you will only hurt you. The other person may not even remember how they hurt you!

Remember that even though these are suggestions for you, there may be times that you will be the person to listen. You will not always be the person in need. That being said, what will you do the next time someone needs to talk about something that is bothering them? And how will you approach others when you need guidance?

The Journey Continues

Things to Think About

Life throws us into many situations, and it is sometimes difficult to remember that we are each one person trying to just make it through life. We each have challenges, whether it is physical, mental, or emotional. And many people go through similar situations, so we are never truly alone, although sometimes we may feel this way. It can be especially difficult to get through stressful situations, but we do not have to do it all on our own. Opening up to a friend or confidant (maybe a counselor?) opens up the lines of communication and lets the other person know that you trust them enough to talk to them. Being alone can be very lonely, but it doesn't have to be. By building relationships—and not just the romantic type—we bring in a network of those we trust, much like a boss sets up a team of those he trusts with certain projects. Building the relationships that you need in life can be a real challenge, but you will be better for it if you can find one or two people that you really trust.

Accepting ourselves as we are, warts and all, has to happen before we even begin the journey. If we do not accept ourselves, then how can others accept us? We need to accept the past and build ourselves up. How do we begin this journey of acceptance? We must first reflect on the things that we like and don't like about ourselves. Unfortunately we all have things about us that we do not like, but when we see something we do not like about ourselves, we have the power to change that part within us, to become what we truly want to be. We need to then change what we can, and accept what we cannot change. We may not be able to change a permanent injury, but we can accept that it is a part of us, work on making improvements within ourselves. Remember that it is difficult for others to accept the physical and mental changes within us, even if we do improve ourselves later on. Then we can work on building relationships with those who have similar ideas while also pursuing friendships that make us think about why we believe the ways that we do.

Building relationships helps us to become healthier mentally and physically. That being said, though, there are also people who are toxic to our health and well-being, and those people should be eliminated from our lives. They are not helping us to get and remain healthy. Having friends to talk to, people to share interests with, helps to keep you focused on what you need. Figure out what you enjoy, what you like to do. Writing helps me to relax, to think clearly, to become more true to myself. What helps you to do that? It could be running, lifting weights, welding, or making things out of wood. Doing something creative allows us to focus on the one activity, keep us thinking of better ways to do something. For example, as I have been writing this book, I have been editing, putting paragraphs in different places, experimenting with wording, and trying to get the information to you in the most readable context. Focusing on the gift that you have, that talent, allows you to focus and improve on whatever that gift is.

Biblical Study

Prayer is important because in praying you are giving your concerns, your worries to God. There are different types of prayer. We all know about prayers of petition, when we are asking for help regarding our wants. We can also pray for guidance. After giving your concerns to God, you are able to focus on the parts of your life that you can control while letting go of those that you cannot control. My mother (God bless her soul), whenever I told her about something that was going on in my life, would tell me to pray about it. I never truly understood until years later what praying about the situation would help with, but her advice stands to this day, that giving your concerns to God is what you need to do when you cannot control the situation.

Prayers of thanksgiving are also appropriate when something good has happened in your life, but thank God for the challenges you are having as well, because those challenges will make you a stronger person. I have friends who are struggling to accept things that have happened in the past, such as physical disabilities, forms of abuse, and other challenges. A lot of times they will ask "Why me? Why did this happen to me?" But it is better to focus on the situation in a different way, asking yourself "Why not me?" By changing the focus we are then able to think of the situation in a less dismal, more hopeful way. Growing up I said why me many times. Why did I go through the windshield? Why did I get a learning disability? Why couldn't I understand something? I finally changed my mindset when I began seeing how I was helping others through using my injury in a more positive manner. I now ask myself "Why not me?"

Here are a few Bible passages that have helped me on my journey of acceptance:

Do not let your hearts be troubled. You have faith in God; have faith also in me (John 14:1; NABRE).

I will not leave you orphans; I will come to you (John 14:18; NABRE).

I can do all this through him who gives me strength (Philippians 4:13; NIV).

Do not fear: I am with you; do not be anxious: I am your God. I will strengthen you, I will help you, I will uphold you with my victorious right hand (Isaiah 41:10; NABRE).

For I am the Lord, your God, who grasp your right hand. It is I who say to you, Do not fear, I will help you (Isaiah 41:13; NABRE).

"Away from me, all who do evil! The Lord has heard the sound of my weeping. The Lord has heard my plea; the Lord will receive my prayer. My foes will all be disgraced and will shudder greatly; they will turn back in sudden disgrace" (Psalm 6:9-11; NABRE).

Keep your chin up, don't stress so much, and tell yourself that you can and will get through the struggle!

Bibliography

American Psychiatric Association: Diagnostic and Statistical Manual of Mental Disorders, Fifth Edition.

Arlington, VA, American Psychiatric Association, 2013.

Umberson, Debra, and Montez, Jennifer Karas (2010). Social Relationships and Health: A Flashpoint for

Health Policy. Journal of Health and Social Behavior, 51 (S), S54-S66.

DOI: 10.1177/0022146510383501

Hollis, Rachel (2018). Girl, Wash Your Face. Nelson Books: Nashville, TN.

Rubin, Gretchen (2017). *7 Types of Loneliness, and Why It Matters.* www.psychologytoday.com

Rubin, Gretchen (2016). *Lonely? 5 Habits to Consider to Combat Loneliness.* www.gretchinrubin.com.

Rubin, Gretchen (2009). *Some Counter-Intuitive Facts About Loneliness.* www.gretchenrubin.com.

The Power of Acceptance. www.abundanceandhappiness.com.

www.kindovermatter.com.

Seltzer, Leon F. (2018). *The Path to Unconditional Self-Acceptance.* www.psychologytoday.com.

Joshi, Shriya (2015). *11 Differences Between Being Alone and Being Lonely*. www.storypick.com.

www.lonerwolf.com.

www.thoughtco.com.

Thoburn, John. *Acceptance: The Foundation of Lasting Relationships*. www.psychologytoday,com.

Meyer, Joyce (2012). <u>Do Yourself a Favor...Forgive</u>. New York, NY: FaithWords, a division of

Hachette Book Group.

Mendes, Wendy Berry, McCoy, Shannon, Major, Brenda, and Blascovich, Jim (2008). How Attributional

Ambiguity Shapes Physiological and Emotional Responses to Social Rejection and Acceptance.

Journal of Personality and Social Psychology, 94 (2), Feb 2008, 278-291.

DOI: 10.1037/0022-3514.94.2.278

DeWall, C. Nathan, and Bushman, Brad J. (2011). Social Acceptance and Rejection: The Sweet and the

Bitter. Current directions in Psychological Science, 20 (4), 256-260.

DOI: 10.1177/0963721411417545

Harris, Holly. *8 Differences Between Loving Someone and Being In Love*. www.Bolde.com.

Ge, Lixia, Yap;, Chun Wei, Ong, Reuben, and Heng, Bee Hoon (2017). Social Isolation, Loneliness, and

Their Relationships with Depressive Symptoms: A Population-Based Study. PLoS One 12(8), 1-

13: e0182145.

DOI: 10.1371/journal.pone.0182145

Gittelman, Maya. *10 Ways to Know When Love Isn't Love: Stay Away from People who Make You Feel*

Like You're Hard to Love. www.thebodyisnotanapology.com.

Anapol, Deborah. *What is Love and What Isn't?* www.psychologytoday.com.

What Love is Not. www.raptitude.com.

Morano, Hara Estroff (2003). *The Dangers of Loneliness.* www.psychologytoday.com.

Winch, Guy (2014). *10 Surprising Facts About Loneliness.* www.psychologytoday.com.

Winch, Guy (2013). *10 Surprising Facts About Rejection.* www.psychologytoday.com.

Winch, Guy (2014). *10 Things You Didn't Know About Self-Esteem.* www.psychologytoday.com.

Glasser, William (1984). Control Theory: A New Explanation of How We Control Our Lives. Harper &

Row: New York, NY.

Patram, Keenan. *Why People Reject Us and What We Can Do About It*. www.tinybuddha.com.

Milburn, Joshua Fields, and Nicodemus, Ryan. *Understanding Others*. www.theminimalists.com.

Pogosyan, Marianna (2016). *Understanding Others*. www.psychologytoday.com.

Leary, Mark R. (2015). Emotional Responses to Interpersonal Rejection. Dialogues of Clinical

Neuroscience, 17 (4), 435-441.

Morin, Amy (2015). *5 Ways Mentally Strong People Deal With Rejection*. www.inc.com.

Williams, Jennifer A. (2018). *Self-Acceptance is the Key to Authentic Power*.

www.blog.hearmanity.com

Bruneau, Megan. *5 Things Everyone Should Know About Acceptance*. www.mindbodygreen.com.

www.pamf.org

www.mentalhealth.org.uk

www.powerofpositivity.com

www.dictionary.com

Mackay, Harvey (2011). *6 Ways to Conquer the Fear of Rejection*. www.inc.com.

Ahuja, Karishma (2018). *6 Ways to Overcome Rejections*. www.entrepreneur.com.

Scott, Elizabeth (2018), *The Top 10 Self-Care Strategies for Stress Reduction*. www.verywellmind.com

Fritscher, Lisa (2018). *Fear of Rejection Behaviors and Consequences*.

www.verywellmind.com.

Lickerman, Alex (2010). *The Six Reasons People Attempt Suicide*.

www.psychologytoday.com.

Sharp, Katie (2012). A Review of Acceptance and Commitment Therapy with Anxiety

Disorders. International Journal of Psychology & Psychological Therapy, 12 (3), 359-

372.

Ducasse, Deborah, Rene, Eric, Beziat, Severine, Guillaume, Sebastien, Courtet, Philippe, and

Olie, Emilie (2014). Acceptance and Commitment Therapy for Management of suicidal

Patients: A Pilot Study. Psychotherapy and Psychosomatics, 83, 374-376.

www.positivepsychologyprogram.com/act-acceptance-and-commitment-therapy

www.goodtherapy.org/learn-about-therapy/issues/rejection

Staple, Maddy. *Why can emotional pain feel physical?* www.sciencefocus.com

Wood, Janice (2018). *Rejection Seems to Hurt Depressed People Longer.*

www.psychcentral.com

Hall, Karyn (2013; blog). *The Emotionally Sensitive Person: Rejection Sensitivity.*

www.psychcentral.com/emotionally-sensitive/2013/05/rejection-sensitivity

Negative Coping to Stress, Trauma, and PTSD (2017). www.spacioustherapy.com

21 Coping Mechanisms to Get You Through the Tough Times. www.morningsiderecovery.com

Rankin, Lissa, MD (March 31, 2011). *11 Natural Treatments for Depression: An MD's Tips for*

Skipping the Prozac. www.psychologytoday.com.

DeMichiel, Sylvia (3/1/2018). *4 Ways to Handle Rejection When you Live With Anxiety and Depression.*

www.TheMighty.com

Schwartz, Allan. *Rejection, Why Does It Hurt So Much?* www.MentalHelp.net.

Glasser, William (1998). Choice Theory. HarperCollins Publishers: New York, NY

Garcy, Pamela D. (2019). *Gracefully Reframing Rejection.* www.psychologytoday.com

www.vantagepointrecovery.com/laughter-mental-health

Davies, Janey. *How to Boost Your Dopamine Function to Beat Your Fears, Anxiety, and*

Depression. www.lifeadvancer.com/dopamine-function

Holy Bible, New International Version (NIV) (2011). Grand Rapids, MI: Zondervan.

The Catholic Youth Bible, Third Edition (2012) (New American Bible, Revised Edition).

Winona, MN: St. Mary's Press.

Pegues, Deborah Smith (2007). 30 Days to Taming Your Stress. Eugene, Oregon: Harvest

House Publishers.

www.beliefnet.com

Brown, Lachlan (January 17, 2019). *How to Love Yourself: 15 Steps to Believing in Yourself*

Again. www.hackspirit.com/how-to-love-yourself

Firestone, Robert. *The Simple Truth About Anger*. www.psychalive.org/simple-truth-anger

McLeod, Lisa Earle (2010). *Anger V. Depression: Two Sides of the Same Coin*.

www.mcleodandmore.com/2010/07/19/angervdepression

Santos-Longhurst, Adrienne (2019). *Do I Have Anger Issues? How to Identify and Treat an*

Angry Outlook. www.healthline.com/health/anger-issues.

Nauert, Rick (2018). *Rejection and Sense of Failure Can Lead to Suicide*.

www.psychcentral.com/news/2014/02/27/rejection-and-sense-of-failure

Compiled by Matthew Kelly through The Dynamic Catholic Institute & Kakadu, LLC..

Beautiful Hope: Finding Hope Every Day in a Broken World. North Palm Beach,

Florida: Beacon Publishing.

Pisegna, C.P., Fr. Cedric. <u>You Can Change: Cooperating With Grace</u>. Chico, CA: Jim and

Janice Carleton.

Cifu, David (February 8, 2017). *Repetitive Head Injury Syndrome*.

www.brainline.org/article/repetitive-head-injury

Hale, Megan. *10 Ways to Forgive Yourself & Let Go of The Past*. www.mindbodygreen.com

Brenner, Abigail, MD (August 29, 2016). *8 Things the Most Toxic People in Your Life Have in*

Common. www.psychologytoday.com

Brown, Lachlan (June 17, 2017). *15 Common Traits of Toxic People, According to*

Psychologists. www.ideapod.com

Peterson, May (July2, 2019). *10 Ways to Let Go of a Toxic Relationship*. www.crosswalk.com

Anger Management Skills (2012). www.therapistaid.com

Deffenbacher, Jerry L., Oetting, Eugene R., and DiGiuseppe, Raymond A. (2002). *Principles of*

Empirically Supported Interventions Applied to Anger Management. The Counseling

Psychologist (30:262-280).

Sheen, Fulton J. (1955). Way to Inner Peace. Garden City, NY: Garden City Books, affiliate of

Doubleday & Company.

Shiel Jr., William C. (2018). *Medical Definition of Grief.* www.medicinenet.com

Gregory, Christina (2019). *The Five Stages of Grief: An Examination of the Kubler-Ross*

Model. www.psycom.net/depression.central.grief.html

Johnson, Jo (May 2, 2019). *Is Frustration and Anger the Same Thing?*

www.angermanagementexpert.co.uk/frustration-anger

Smith, Kathleen (November 25, 2018). *When Anger Becomes Emotional Abuse: How to*

Control Anger and Frustration in a Relationship. www.psycom.net/control-anger-

frustration-relationship

Taylor, Jane. *6 Core Human Needs by Anthony Robbins.* www.habitsforwellbeing.com

Langslet, Kari. 3 Signs a Toxic Person is Manipulating You (And What to Do About It).

www.greatist.com

West, Mary (2022). Maslow's Hierarchy of Needs: Uses and Criticisms. www.medicalnewstody.com

www.ingramcontent.com/pod-product-compliance
Lightning Source LLC
Chambersburg PA
CBHW071440120125
20249CB00013B/1055